NEIGHBORHOOD

HEARTY SALADS AND PLANT-BASED RECIPES FROM HOME AND ABROAD

HETTY MCKINNON

Photography by Luisa Brimble

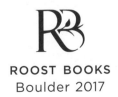

ROOST BOOKS
Boulder 2017

For Ross, Scout, Dash, and Huck ~ for being the people I like to feed the most xx

CONTENTS

INTRODUCTION

MAKING FRIENDS WITH SALAD

My unconventional journey in salad-making began in 2011, when I established a community kitchen in my inner city home in Sydney, Australia. Twice every week, I would cook healthy and hearty plant-based salad boxes, stack them into my bicycle basket, and deliver them to locals. I called my adventure Arthur Street Kitchen.

What started as a simple desire to share my favorite vegetable-laden salads with my local community yielded unexpected results. As I traversed the laneways and climbed the hills of my neighborhood Surry Hills, I witnessed a movement that centered upon so much more than food. In the hunting and gathering of stories and histories with local salad-eaters, I saw the importance of food in allowing people to feel connected with others. Because of that, my neighborhood, and the people within it, have become a very big influence on the way I cook and my approach to food.

In my time as a cook, sharing food has become a vehicle for establishing new friendships and building meaningful connections in my neighborhood. It is humbling to realize that even among the hustle of our modern lives, simple acts like cooking for others, eating together, and sharing food are sentiments that still resonate strongly.

In late 2014, my husband and I packed up our three children, bid adieu to our beloved neighborhood of Surry Hills, and headed north. We landed in France and ate our way through the local Provençal markets. We introduced our children to the sights, sounds, and tastes of Italy, Germany, Finland, and our old "hometown" of London. Finally, we ended our trip in Brooklyn, New York, where the next chapter of our lives and Arthur Street Kitchen began.

REINVENTING VEGETABLES
Salads allow me to express my love for my other great passion—vegetables. At the heart of every one of my salads is a core seasonal vegetable—from there, the dish can venture virtually anywhere! Add a grain for heartiness, inject some herbs for freshness, incorporate some spice for intrigue, and finish with a nut for crunch. The possibilities are endless.

Having been vegetarian for over half my life, my belief in a plant-based diet as the ideal way to eat is unerring. But this book does not make statements about vegetarianism. Rather, it is my aim to encourage home cooks to think more creatively about vegetables, understand their versatility, and cook them with more confidence and flair. In my view, when given the right treatment and thought, there is nothing more delicious or satisfying than a flavor-packed, vegetable-based salad.

Neighborhood will show home cooks that you don't have to be a vegetarian to enjoy vegetables, and you don't have to be a chef to be a good cook.

THE BIG VEGETABLE SALAD

It is reasonable to say that I am rather enamored with salads. It is by far my favorite dish to eat. No matter what flavor you are pining for, or what ingredient you are craving, you can incorporate it spectacularly into a salad. For me, salads allow me to be creative, embracing the thrilling myriad of flavors, textures, ingredients, and fresh seasonal produce that come from living in a multicultural world.

My salads are not the lettuce-based, leafy varieties you may be accustomed to. The recipes in this book elevate the salad from side dish to main meal. Using vegetables as their life force, my salads are the main event, not the support act. *Neighborhood* aims to inspire readers to look at vegetable salads in a new light, giving cooks the confidence to prepare delicious and hearty meals with the feel of comfort food, without the need for meat.

ALL THE WORLD'S NEIGHBORHOODS

Neighborhood is a collection of salad recipes inspired by "places," journeying from Brooklyn in New York to the greater Americas, the Mediterranean, Asia, France, my native Australia, and many other places around the world for salad-making inspiration.

If community is a feeling of kinship, *Neighborhood* is a physical compilation of the sights, sounds, and colors of a geographic area. Growing up in Australia, living in London, and traveling extensively through Europe before settling in brownstone Brooklyn, I have been continually drawn to the role of food as a social anchor in a neighborhood. No matter where you live in the world, it is the daily rituals of eating that strongly influence the way we live. It is the places I visit regularly—from grabbing a cream cheese bagel at my corner bodega, picking up fresh mozzarella from the local deli, or stopping by the greenmarket for seasonal produce—that have inspired my latest salad-making adventures, with exciting new international flavors and bold new vegetable pairings.

THE NEIGHBORHOOD

It can be said that New York City is a city of neighborhoods. Each has their own unique personality, forged from history and circumstance. Often, entire neighborhoods are founded on the culture of food. From the Chinatowns of Lower Manhattan, Sunset Park in Brooklyn, and Flushing in Queens to Koreatown around 32nd Street, the Little Italies in Manhattan, and Bensonhurst in Brooklyn, the curry and spice emporiums of Murray Hill, the colorful Indian and Pakistani food in Jackson Heights, the old-world Russian delicacies in Brighton Beach, and Greek and Egyptian treats in Astoria, culinary neighborhoods like these are the beating heart of New York City.

When we put down roots in Carroll Gardens, a charismatic neighborhood of deep-fronted brownstones and a robust Italo–American background in south Brooklyn, I was struck by the strength of history in the area. Over the last few decades, Carroll Gardens, like many Brooklyn neighborhoods, has undergone a cultural makeover. With that, many of the old local haunts have closed their doors or moved deeper into the suburbs. But still, amid the urban evolution, there remains a strong sense of neighborhood in the area. Italian flags fly alongside American ones, ubiquitous Virgin Mary statues adorn front and back yards, while old-school delicatessens, pizzerias, and enotecas still stand amongst the slick new wine bars and sleekly designed restaurants. This is an area with a strong narrative and a tenacious sense of its past, present, and future.

A fundamental part of this neighborhood story is in the local food. My local Italian deli, Caputo's Fine Foods, has been a neighborhood institution for over four decades, a family-owned store where the owner makes fresh mozzarella (several times a day!), and supplies fresh and dried pasta, antipasti, olive oils, and more. Up the street, an unrelated bakery that happens to share the same name, Caputo's Bake Shop, has been supplying the neighborhood with baked goods since the early 1900s. The ciabatta, especially the olive-encrusted one, is my essential daily bread and their pizza dough is a family staple. Unassuming brick-fronted pizzerias owned by long-time locals still serve up crispy-based, cheesy-topped pizza pies to residents, old and new. On Sundays, the Carroll Gardens Greenmarket thrills me with the color of seasonal produce grown at farms nearby; most weeks, I still discover a fruit or vegetable that is unfamiliar to me. And in between, daily visits to my favorite local bodega, Sue's Organics, bring me reliably sourced produce and lively conversation.

In making Brooklyn home, it has been these humble, everyday neighborhood haunts that have given me a tangible sense of belonging and connection. Through the hunting and gathering of food, I am gradually becoming a local.

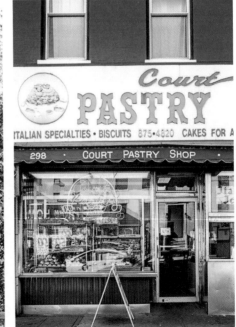

WEEKNIGHT SALADS

If I had my choice, I would always advocate slow cooking. For me, one of life's great luxuries is to take the time to shop for the freshest ingredients, cook real food from scratch, and share meals with family, friends, and neighbors. However, I also appreciate that weeknight meals are often about being quick and easy. One of the most common questions I am asked is how to make a salad quickly. My best advice on speedy salad making: GET PREPARED!

Here I've thrown together a few practical ideas on how to make your weeknight salad prep a bit easier and quicker.

ON THE WEEKEND, STOCK YOUR PANTRY

Let's be honest, having a thoughtfully stocked pantry is your first step to simplifying your weekly cooking. My confession here is that I'm a food hoarder. I love buying food items, even if I'm not in immediate need. You just never know, right? My friends used to joke that if we were faced with war and famine, they would bunker down at my house because my food stocks would keep us fed for months. But in my madness, there is some method. Getting into the habit of picking up a few essentials on a weekly basis will allow you to gradually build up your pantry stocks, inevitably making last-minute cooking a whole lot easier.

On the weekends (or whenever you do your major household shop), stock up on basics you will need for the week. Here are some tips on how to stock your pantry, fridge, and freezer for quicker and easier salad making:

Choose two or three main seasonal vegetables for the week
Picking up many different types of vegetables can make weekday cooking confusing. Instead, just pick two or three vegetables that are in season, inexpensive, and look delicious. These vegetables can be the centerpiece of your meal, so instead of buying one cauliflower, buy two or three of them.

Pick two types of soft herbs to see you through the week
My favorites to have in the fridge are parsley, cilantro, mint, and green onions (see note page 32). These herbs are very flexible, can be used in a range of dishes, and will really transform your salads.

Stock up on canned legumes
Great choices are chickpeas, borlotti beans, butter beans, black beans, and cannellini beans. If you have a can of beans, a vegetable, and herbs, you virtually have a salad right there!

Make grains pantry staples

Stored in airtight jars, they keep for months and they are great to add bulk to your dish. I always have quinoa, pearl barley, and bulgur wheat (cracked wheat) in my pantry as I find them so versatile and, importantly, quick to cook!

Stock your freezer with a few essentials

My freezer essentials are edamame beans, garden peas, and lotus root.

CHOP IT UP

If you have a spare half hour on the weekend, chop up your veggies, ready for cooking. If you have kale, remove the stems and tear up the leaves. For vegetables like cauliflower or broccoli, cut them into florets and keep the stalks separate. Store everything in airtight plastic containers or ziplock bags and keep in the vegetable drawer of your refrigerator to keep crisp. This small step will make weekday cooking so much quicker. (Note: this only applies to vegetables that won't oxidize and turn brown when cooked, so a definite no to vegetables like potato, eggplant, and artichokes.)

COOK IN ADVANCE

Roast, barbecue, grill, or pan-fry your vegetables in advance and keep them in the refrigerator. Most vegetables, without sauce or flavor added, will keep in an airtight container in the refrigerator for 1–2 days.

MAKE TOASTED NUTS AND SEEDS A PANTRY STAPLE

Toast a variety of nuts and seeds in bulk and keep them in airtight jars in your pantry. I usually have jars of toasted walnuts, almonds, peanuts, pistachios, and sesame seeds ready in my pantry.

PRE-COOK A GRAIN

Consider cooking one or two grains in advance and keeping them in the refrigerator, ready for salad assembly. Quinoa keeps well in the fridge for 5–6 days, and can even be frozen for up to 6 months. Other grains that you could cook in advance are pearl barley, spelt, farro, freekeh, and brown rice.

FRIDGE AND FREEZER DRESSINGS

Dressings can be made in advance, and either stored in the refrigerator or freezer. Vinaigrettes, flavored yogurts, or versatile Asian-style dressings are fine to store in the fridge for 2–3 days. Pesto and scented oils can be frozen for up to 3 months. Just make sure to bring the dressings back to room temperature before using.

FOUR WAYS TO USE LEFTOVER SALAD

In my house, there is often a plethora of leftover salad. The Chinese in me always has me cooking for the masses. So over the years, I have devised a few interesting, delicious ways to use up leftover salad. I thought I'd share these with you.

1. PUT AN EGG ON IT

When in doubt, put a fried egg on it.

Sometimes, if the salad is robust enough to do so, I like to quickly fry the leftovers in a little extra-virgin olive oil, just to add some heat, then top the whole thing off with a fried egg. Just like that, you have a hearty lunch or light dinner.

2. BLEND IT INTO A SOUP

I love blending leftover salad, transforming it into a hearty soup.

Simply throw your leftover salad into a food processor or blender, add a cup of vegetable broth or liquid vegetable stock and blend the whole mix up. This salad do-over is perfect for those salads without too many leaves and which are heavy on legumes or roasted vegetables. If you have a lot of leftovers, you can even freeze the soup for later consumption.

3. MAKE A GRILLED CHEESE

A grilled cheese is the perfect anytime and every time meal. This type of sandwich is serious business—especially in the United States where there is great pride taken in a perfect grilled cheese. Use a sandwich grill if you have one, but here, I show you how to make the perfect grilled cheese sandwich using your everyday frying pan:

Take two thick slices of sourdough bread or ciabatta.

Spread butter on both sides of both slices of bread (yes, both!).

Layer one side of both slices with whole egg mayonnaise.

Heat a large non-stick frying pan or griddle pan over medium-low heat and add the bread slices (mayonnaise-side down) to cook. Slide them around the pan to achieve an even golden color.

Flip them both over, then pile one slice with leftover salad, and top with your favorite melty cheese—try cheddar, Swiss, gruyere, mozzarella, provolone, brie—and place the other slice of bread on the top, browned-side down (you want the uncooked sides on the outside). »

Cook the sandwich, moving it around the pan to get an even browning, for about 2 minutes on each side.

A grilled cheese sandwich is fantastic made with roasted broccoli, cauliflower, carrots, sweet potato, and, my favorite, brussels sprouts.

---

4. GO KUKU!

Turning a salad into a kuku is perhaps my very favorite way of embracing leftovers.

Kuku is a rather exotic name for an Iranian-inspired frittata, laced with a subtle hit of saffron, and perfect served at room temperature. Over the years, I have made this dish countless times using leftover salads—it is great with roasted vegetable salads, but also works wonderfully with legumes and grain salads with bulgur wheat, spelt, and barley.

SERVES 4~6

3 tablespoons extra-virgin olive oil
2 onions, halved and finely sliced
1 garlic clove, finely chopped
6 eggs
2 tablespoons all-purpose flour
1 teaspoon baking powder
small pinch of saffron threads, soaked in 1 tablespoon boiling water
4 cups leftover salad
3 tablespoons chopped soft herbs (parsley, dill, mint, cilantro, chives, etc.)
½ pomegranate, seeds extracted
sea salt and black pepper

Preheat the oven to 350°F (180°C). Line a 9 in (22 cm) springform pan with parchment paper.

In a large frying pan, heat the olive oil and fry the onions and garlic for 7–8 minutes, or until the onions are soft and starting to caramelize. Allow to cool.

In a mixing bowl, add the eggs and whisk until smooth. Add the flour, baking powder, saffron and its soaking water, sea salt, and a good grind of black pepper, and whisk until smooth.

In the springform pan, lay out the onions, then spoon over the leftover salad. Pour over the egg mixture. Place the pan on a large baking tray (to catch any leaks) and bake in the oven for 45–50 minutes until golden and the egg is set. Insert a skewer to make sure the kuku is cooked all the way through.

To serve, scatter over the soft herbs and pomegranate seeds. Serve warm, or at room temperature. The kuku will keep in the refrigerator for 2–3 days.

COOK'S NOTES

COOK YOUR BEANS WITH SALT AND GARLIC!

Like most people, as a young cook, I was taught never to add salt to the cooking water for legumes, lest we end up with hard-skinned, inedible beans. But one day, I decided to experiment—I added a big pinch of salt at the beginning of cooking my beans, along with a clove of peeled garlic. The result? I have never looked back!

I have found that salting the bean cooking water helps them cook faster, adds so much flavor, makes the beans taste creamier, and helps them stay much more intact! The fact is, beans are fairly tempestuous beings. You do need to play around with cooking methods and times to get things right. But I encourage you to persist because the results are truly worth it. In fact, many varieties of beans like borlotti, cannellini, black-eyed peas, and butter beans don't take that long to cook—about 40–45 minutes from start to finish. Chickpeas take a little longer, about 1 hour (depending on how fresh the dried chickpeas are—older chickpeas take a long time to cook and sometimes never soften fully). I don't even bother to soak them overnight, but soaking does speed up the cooking time.

How to: Cover your beans in plenty of water. Bring to a boil, and allow to cook on high heat for about 5 minutes. Turn the heat down to a low simmer, add two or three big pinches of sea salt and one clove of garlic. Cook until the beans are tender. At the end of cooking, the garlic should either be disintegrated, or will break up with a little stirring. Drain.

COOK YOUR GRAINS IN FLAVOR

Making a salad is about building layers of subtle flavors. At every opportunity, I inject flavor into each ingredient of the salad. So when cooking grains like pearl barley, spelt, farro, freekeh, quinoa, or rice, using vegetable stock or well-salted water will add so much more flavor to the final dish.

ALLOW GRAINS TO SIT AND FLUFF UP

After cooking grains like quinoa, bulgur wheat (cracked wheat), and couscous, give them 10 minutes or so to sit and "dry out" slightly. I like to turn the stovetop off and leave the pot on the hot element to just allow the residual steam to evaporate naturally. This will leave you with fluffier grains.

ALWAYS EAT SALADS AT ROOM TEMPERATURE

If I was to give lessons about how to eat a salad, this would be my number one piece of advice—eat your salad at room temperature. With the exception of chilled dishes like soba noodles, I recommend eating all salads at room temperature to experience optimum flavor.

THE GOOD OIL

Unless otherwise specified, when I refer to oil, I'm talking about extra-virgin olive oil. In most cases, I use extra-virgin olive oil for the cooking of vegetables, along with dressings. This is purely out of convenience, as I don't often have many different types of oil in the kitchen. For me, extra-virgin olive oil is perfect on most foods! If you prefer a lighter oil, you can use standard olive oil or even a neutral oil like grapeseed.

For ease and clarity, I indicate how much olive oil will be required for a particular recipe. But I encourage you to use your own discretion. Some people love their food drenched in olive oil, and if this is the case, please do so! If you are cutting back on oily food, then use less. This is your call.

THE ONION ISSUE

A spring onion is a shallot is a green onion or scallion! No, they are NOT all the same thing. To further complicate the issue, they are known by different names all around the United States. In this cookbook, for the sake of clarity, the image opposite shows you precisely what I am referring to when I use the terms green onion, spring onion, and shallot.

RECIPE NOTES

Cups and spoons of herbs and greens (like arugula, spinach, kale, etc.) are always TIGHTLY PACKED.

I always use Maldon sea salt flakes.

For parsley, I only use the flat-leaf (continental) variety.

Black pepper is better freshly ground.

Be liberal and flexible with quantities, especially with your vegetables. As this is salad-making and not baking, exact, precise quantities and measurements are not essential. So don't fret over the size of your cauliflower or sweet potato. Think about how many people you are cooking for and adjust the recipe accordingly! Leftovers are perfect for lunch the next day, sharing with friends and neighbors or perhaps trying my leftover salad ideas on page 26.

I've included symbols for dishes that are gluten free (GF) and vegan (VG).

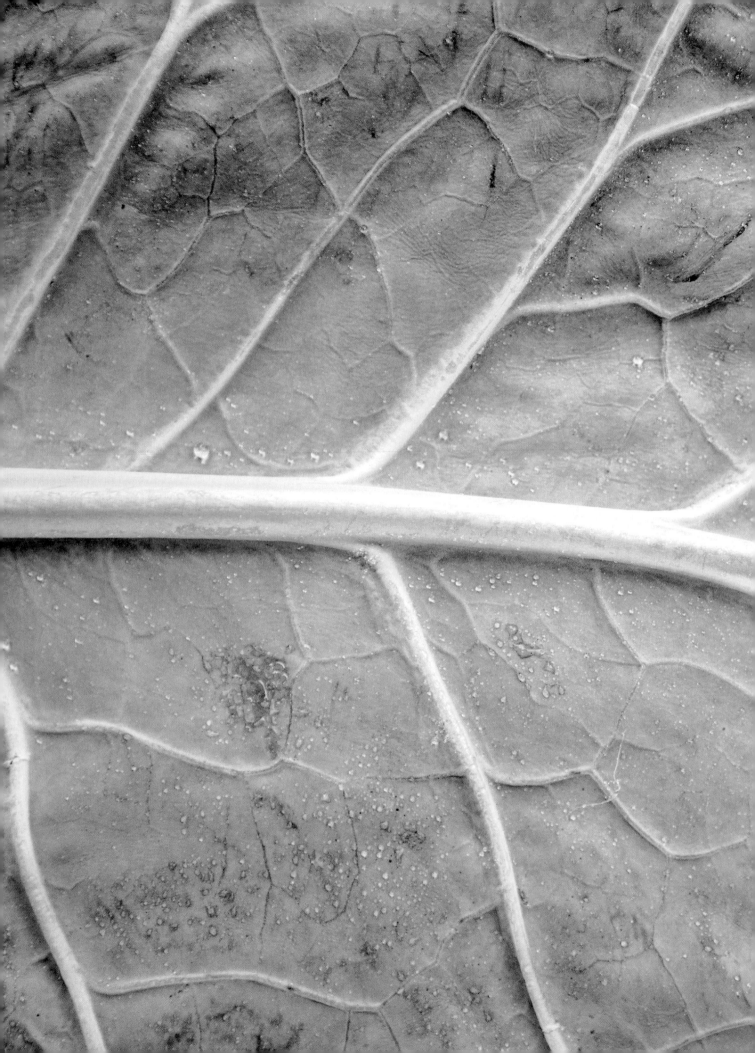

DEAR AMERICA

Like the country and its people, the food in America is vast, diverse, passionate and bold. As I find my culinary feet in my adopted home neighborhood of Brooklyn, it has been wonderful to meet the comforting flavors from the South, to be swept along with the lively Mexican wave, and to embrace the fusion flavors of Latin cuisine. To live in New York City is to truly have the world's food at your front door, at whatever time of the day! Here, food fads are born and disseminated across the globe. Food is theater, a full-bodied experience designed to entertain and challenge all your senses.

SHREDDED COLLARD GREENS, BAKED SWEET POTATO, AND PINTO BEANS WITH PAPRIKA-BUTTERMILK DRESSING

Collard greens, with their deep green, thick leaves, stand up to lengthy cooking times, while still retaining their flavor and texture. For me, however, I also love them raw. For this salad, I'm celebrating the Southern roots of collard greens by teaming them with roast sweet potato, pinto beans, and a spicy buttermilk dressing. I've written this recipe with substitutions for both collard greens and pinto beans for a variation on this dish.

GF | SERVES 4~6

3 sweet potatoes (about 1½ lbs; 700 g), unpeeled and cut into ½ in (1 cm) cubes
3–4 tablespoons extra-virgin olive oil
1 bunch of collard greens (about 14 oz; 400 g), washed and stems removed
One and one half 15 oz cans (500 g) pinto beans (about 2 cups), drained
⅓ cup cilantro leaves
½ cup sunflower seeds, toasted
1 lime, cut into wedges
Sea salt and black pepper

PAPRIKA-BUTTERMILK DRESSING

¾ cup (185 ml) buttermilk
3 tablespoons sour cream
1 garlic clove, very finely chopped
1 teaspoon paprika
½ teaspoon smoked paprika
Juice of ½ lime
1 tablespoon extra-virgin olive oil
Sea salt and black pepper

SUBSTITUTES

Collard greens: cavolo nero, kale
Pinto beans: red kidney beans, borlotti beans

Preheat the oven to 400°F (200°C).

Place the sweet potato pieces on a large baking tray, toss them in 2 tablespoons of olive oil and season with salt and pepper. Roast for 20–25 minutes until tender.

Slice the collard green leaves very finely using a sharp knife and place them in a large bowl. Drizzle over 1–2 tablespoons of olive oil, add a pinch of salt, and massage the oil into the leaves for about a minute (this will start to soften the leaves).

To make the buttermilk dressing, mix together the buttermilk and sour cream in a bowl and stir in the chopped garlic, paprika, lime juice, and olive oil. Season with salt and pepper.

Combine the massaged leaves with the sweet potato, beans, cilantro, and sunflower seeds. Season again with salt and pepper, spoon over the buttermilk dressing, and serve with the lime wedges on the side.

ROASTED GOLDEN BEETS WITH LENTILS, SOFT HERBS, AND LEMON-SAFFRON YOGURT

While golden beets are often near impossible to find in some parts of the world, they are excitingly abundant during the New York summer. Slightly less earthy and mellower than their crimson-hued equals, golden beets are like a ray of sunshine. This salad is exactly that—sunshine on a plate. The roasted beets are enlivened with a bounty of fresh herbs and a sunny lemon and saffron yogurt.

GF | SERVES 4~6

8 golden beets (about 3½ lbs; 1.6 kg),
    peeled and cut into ½ in (1 cm) cubes
3–4 tablespoons extra-virgin olive oil
1 tablespoon white balsamic vinegar
2 cups (400 g) brown lentils, rinsed
2 cups soft herb leaves (parsley, dill,
    cilantro, chives, mint, oregano,
    or tarragon)
Sea salt and black pepper

LEMON-SAFFRON YOGURT

Pinch of saffron strands
1½ cups (375 g) Greek yogurt
2 tablespoons extra-virgin olive oil
Squeeze of lemon juice
Sea salt and black pepper

SUBSTITUTES

Golden beets: red or target beets

Preheat the oven to 400°F (200°C).

Place the beets on a large baking tray, drizzle over 2–3 tablespoons of olive oil and the white balsamic vinegar. Season well with salt and pepper and roast for 30–35 minutes, or until the beets are tender.

Place the lentils in a saucepan and cover with plenty of cold water. Add a big pinch of salt. Bring to a boil, reduce to a simmer, and cook for 20–25 minutes or until just tender. Drain.

To make the lemon-saffron yogurt, place the saffron strands in a small bowl and pour over 2 tablespoons of boiling water. Allow to steep for 10 minutes. When ready, add the yogurt to the saffron and water and stir to combine. Add the olive oil, squeeze in the lemon juice, and season well with salt and pepper.

To serve, combine the beets with the lentils and all the herbs. Fold the yogurt through, season with salt and pepper, and finish with a drizzle of olive oil.

CHIMICHURRI SALAD BOWL WITH EGGPLANT, TOFU, FENNEL, AND SHIITAKE MUSHROOMS

There is a lot to admire about chimichurri, an Argentinean paste traditionally used as a rub for meats. It is fiery, herby, tangy, and garlicky, and offers a vibrant tang that is also perfect for marinating vegetables. Here, I've taken chimichurri on an Asian journey, using it as a marinade for eggplant, tofu, and fresh shiitake mushrooms. The yogurt tames the spice. The chimichurri can be made 24 hours ahead and, if you want to get extra prepared, it is also OK to marinate the vegetables in the chimichurri overnight.

GF | SERVES 4~6

2 eggplants (about 1¾ lbs; 800 g)

1 fennel bulb, shaved

14 oz (400 g) firm tofu, cut
    into 1½ in (1 cm) cubes

½ lb (200 g) fresh shiitake mushrooms (or
    other Asian mushroom such as oyster),
    cleaned and trimmed

¾ cup (185 g) Greek yogurt

3 cups (550 g) cooked brown rice

1–2 tablespoons extra-virgin olive oil

½ cup cilantro leaves

3 tablespoons white sesame seeds, toasted

Sea salt and black pepper

CHIMICHURRI (MAKES 1 CUP/250 ML)

2 garlic cloves, very finely chopped

2 teaspoons sea salt

½–1 jalapeño chili

1 teaspoon paprika

1 teaspoon ground cumin

⅓ cup (80 ml) red wine vinegar

1 cup flat-leaf parsley leaves, finely chopped

2 tablespoons oregano leaves

2 tablespoons chopped green onion
    (see note page 32)

1 cup (250 ml) extra-virgin olive oil

SUBSTITUTES/OPTIONS

Eggplant/mushroom/fennel: zucchini,
    carrots, sweet potato, asparagus

For vegans, omit yogurt

To make the chimichurri, place all the ingredients in the bowl of a food processor and whiz it all up. It is up to you how much jalapeño chili you use—I suggest starting with a small portion and adding more as you go along. Alternatively, use a mortar and pestle to grind everything together. Leave to sit for at least 30 minutes, or for up to 24 hours.

Peel strips of skin from the eggplants, from top to bottom, so it leaves a stripy pattern. Cut the flesh into ½ in (1 cm) cubes. Place the eggplant, fennel, tofu, and mushrooms in four separate bowls. Spoon about 1 tablespoon of chimichurri over each, toss to coat, transfer to the refrigerator, and leave to marinate for at least 30 minutes, ideally overnight.

When ready to cook, heat a large frying pan or griddle pan over medium heat with olive oil. Working in batches to avoid overcrowding the pan, fry the eggplant cubes until golden and tender. Remove and allow them to rest in a colander. In the same pan, cook the tofu until golden. Finally, fry the mushrooms until cooked and golden.

To serve, place a dollop of yogurt in the center of a large serving bowl and arrange the eggplant, tofu, mushrooms, brown rice, and raw marinated fennel around it. Spoon over any remaining chimichurri, season with salt and pepper, drizzle with the olive oil, and scatter over the cilantro leaves and sesame seeds.

BEAN CHILI WITH CRISPY TORTILLA STRIPS
AND CREAMY AVOCADO SALSA

Before we arrived in the United States, I didn't quite grasp the pervasive, powerful influence of Mexican-inspired food here. Like in Britain where you "go out for a curry," chili comes close to being the national dish in America. While not necessarily traditional or authentic, chili is actually a blend of Mexican and southern American influences that has worked its way into most local kitchens. In our Brooklyn home, chili is our winter Sunday evening staple, ceremoniously and meticulously prepared by my husband Ross.

GF | SERVES 4~6

3–4 tablespoons extra-virgin olive oil
1 onion, finely diced
1 garlic clove, very finely chopped
2 teaspoons cumin seeds
2 teaspoons paprika
2 teaspoons chipotle powder
2 teaspoons dried oregano
One and one half 15 oz cans (500 g) pinto
    beans (about 2 cups)
One and one half 15 oz cans (500 g) black
    beans (about 2 cups)
One and one half 15 oz cans (500 g) red
    kidney beans (about 2 cups)
½ lb (200 g) cherry tomatoes, halved
2 bell peppers (red, yellow, or 1 of each),
    deseeded and cut into ½ in (1 cm) dice
1 cup cilantro leaves
1 lime, cut into 6 wedges
Sea salt and black pepper

CRISPY TORTILLA STRIPS

6 corn tortillas
1–2 tablespoons sunflower oil
Pinch of sea salt
Small pinch of chipotle powder, mixed
    with a pinch of paprika powder

CREAMY AVOCADO SALSA

2 large avocados (about 600 g), diced
1 tomato, deseeded and finely diced
1 shallot (see note page 32), very finely diced
1 Lebanese cucumber, deseeded and
    finely diced
1 long red chili, deseeded and finely chopped
3 tablespoons natural yogurt
Juice of 1–2 limes
2 tablespoons extra-virgin olive oil
Sea salt

Preheat the oven to 400°F (200°C).

Heat 2 tablespoons of olive oil in a large frying pan over medium heat, add the onion and garlic, and cook for 5 minutes or so, until soft. Add the cumin seeds, paprika, chipotle powder, and oregano and cook for 30 seconds, until fragrant. Drain the beans and add to the pan, drizzle with some more olive oil, season well with salt and pepper, and fry the beans for 6–8 minutes, until they are just starting to get crispy. Remove from the heat and leave to cool completely.

For the crispy tortilla strips, brush each side of the corn tortillas with sunflower oil and stack them on top of each other. Cut them in half, then slice each half into ¼ in (6 mm) strips. Spread them out in a single layer on a large baking tray, sprinkle over the salt and the chipotle and paprika spice mix, and toss gently. Bake for 10–15 minutes, or until crispy.

To make the avocado salsa, put all the ingredients in a bowl and stir to combine. Season with salt, taste, and add extra lime juice if necessary.

To put the salad together, combine the beans with the cherry tomatoes and bell peppers in a large serving bowl. Drizzle over some olive oil, top with the crispy tortilla strips and cilantro, and serve with the avocado salsa and lime wedges on the side.

CHIPOTLE BLACK BEANS WITH COLLARD GREENS, AVOCADO, AND CHIPOTLE-LIME VINAIGRETTE

When I arrive in a new place, one of the first things I do is explore the local supermarket. I love seeing the foreign packaging, the familiar and unfamiliar brands, and discovering new produce. For me, the supermarket shelf is a snapshot of a neighborhood's food culture, habits and rituals. In our early days in Brooklyn, we stayed temporarily in Williamsburg, where the local supermarket shelves were lined with countless chipotle chili products. This dish is an ode to chipotle and my other great American love, collard greens. This salad is smokin' hot.

VG | GF | SERVES 4~6

2–3 tablespoons extra-virgin olive oil
1 garlic clove, very finely chopped
½ red onion, finely diced
1 dried chipotle chili, soaked in boiling
  water for 30 minutes, drained and
  finely chopped
One and one half 15 oz cans (500 g) black
  beans (about 2 cups)
1 bunch of collard greens (about 14 oz;
  400 g), stems removed and very
  finely sliced
2 large avocados (about 21 oz; 600 g), diced
½ cup squash seeds, toasted
½ cup cilantro leaves
Sea salt and black pepper

CHIPOTLE-LIME VINAIGRETTE

1 dried chipotle chili, soaked in boiling
  water for 30 minutes, drained and
  finely chopped
Juice of 1–2 limes
½ cup (125 ml) extra-virgin olive oil
1 teaspoon ground cumin
1 teaspoon superfine sugar
1 garlic clove, very finely chopped
Sea salt and black pepper

SUBSTITUTES

Black beans: red kidney beans
Collard greens: cavolo nero, kale

Heat the olive oil in a large frying pan over medium heat. Add the garlic, onion, and chipotle chili and cook for 2 minutes, then add the black beans, along with a big pinch of salt, and toss well. Continue to cook for 3–4 minutes until the beans are slightly crispy.

To make the chipotle-lime vinaigrette, add the chopped chipotle chili to a bowl with most of the lime juice, olive oil, cumin, sugar, and garlic. Whisk together, adjusting the lime juice until you achieve your preferred acidity. Season with salt and pepper to taste.

Combine the black beans, collard greens, and avocado. Spoon over the chipotle-lime vinaigrette, season well with salt and pepper and toss everything together. To serve, scatter over the squash seeds and cilantro leaves.

SPICED TOFU WITH BLACK BEANS, BARBECUED CORN, AND RED BELL PEPPERS

This recipe is one of many twists and turns. It started off as a scrambled tofu stir-fry, inspired by a Sophie Dahl recipe. But, as with many dishes in my repertoire, it soon morphed into a salad of Tex-Mex influence. The heavily spiced, smoky tofu is really one of my favorite things to eat. My kids love it just as much. Roll it up in a corn tortilla or soft taco shell for a simple, flavor-packed family meal.

VG | GF | SERVES 4~6

2 red bell peppers (about ¾ lb; 350 g)
3 corn cobs (about 1¼ lbs; 550 g)
2–3 tablespoons extra-virgin olive oil
2 shallots (see note page 32), peeled
  and finely diced
1 garlic clove, crushed
28 oz (800 g) firm tofu,
  torn into chunks
½ jalapeño chili, deseeded and
  finely diced
2 teaspoons ground cumin
½ teaspoon ground turmeric
1 teaspoon smoked paprika
One and one half 15 oz cans (500 g) black
  beans (about 2 cups), drained
½ cup cilantro leaves
Juice of 1 lime
Sea salt and black pepper

SUBSTITUTE

Red bell peppers: store-bought
  roasted red peppers

Preheat a griddle pan or barbecue. You need it smoking hot.

Lay the peppers on the pan or barbecue and cook for 10–12 minutes, turning, until blackened on all sides. Place the peppers in a bowl, cover with plastic wrap and leave to steam for 10 minutes. When ready, peel off and discard the charred skin along with the seeds and membrane, and roughly chop the pepper flesh. (To save on time and effort, you can definitely use store-bought roasted red peppers.)

Add the corn cobs to the pan or barbecue and cook on all sides, until slightly charred. Leave them to cool slightly, then run a sharp knife down each side to remove the kernels.

In a large frying pan, add 1–2 tablespoons of olive oil and the shallots and garlic and cook over medium heat until the shallots are translucent. Add the tofu chunks, then the chili, cumin, turmeric, and paprika and move around, making sure the tofu is evenly coated in the spices. Add a big pinch of salt and pepper and cook for 5–6 minutes until the tofu is starting to take on some golden color.

Combine the bell peppers, corn, black beans, tofu mixture, and cilantro and mix well. To serve, squeeze over the lime juice and finish with a drizzle of olive oil.

MUSHROOMS AND KASHA
WITH RAINBOW CHARD AND RADISH

Kasha is another name for roasted buckwheat and it is very popular in Russia and Ukraine where it is one of the oldest known dishes in Central and Eastern European cuisine. I hadn't eaten much kasha over the years, but recently in Little Ukraine in New York City's East Village, I experienced the loveliness of kasha and mushrooms stuffed in cabbage. The dish was so wonderful it got me thinking about the possibilities of kasha and mushrooms as a new salad power couple. Say hi to my "KashRoom" salad. Stay alert when you are cooking kasha as it will quickly turn to mush if you overcook it. The trick is to add the stock a little at a time and taste often to see when the grains are just ready.

GF | SERVES 4~6

2½ cups (400 g) kasha (roasted buckwheat)
3–4 tablespoons extra-virgin olive oil
4 cups (1 liter) vegetable stock
1 garlic clove, very finely chopped
1 lb (400 g) mixed mushrooms
　(any variety), cleaned
½ bunch rainbow chard with stalks
　(about 11 oz; 300 g), finely sliced
1½ tablespoons (20 g) butter
1 cup soft herb leaves (mint,
　cilantro, parsley, or chives)
4 radishes (about 5 oz; 150 g), trimmed
　and very finely sliced
Juice of ½ lemon
Sea salt and black pepper

SUBSTITUTES/OPTIONS

Kasha: pearl barley, quinoa
Rainbow chard: Swiss chard, spinach
For vegans, omit butter

Coat the kasha grains in 1 tablespoon of olive oil and a few big pinches of salt. Mix together well to coat the grains evenly.

In a large shallow frying pan, add the kasha and cook for 20 seconds over medium heat. Add a little stock, stir, and leave to simmer on medium-low heat. When the liquid has been absorbed, add enough stock to cover the kasha grains and continue like this until the kasha has softened enough to eat, but is still a little crunchy. Don't let it cook too long as it will turn to mush. Place the kasha into a bowl.

In the same frying pan, add 1 tablespoon of olive oil and the garlic and cook over medium-high heat for 30 seconds. Add the mushrooms, season with salt and pepper, and cook until all the mushroom juices have evaporated. Add a further 1 tablespoon of olive oil along with the chard stalks and cook for 60 seconds. Finally, add the chard leaves and cook for another 30 seconds or so, just long enough to wilt the leaves. Take off the heat and add the butter to the mushrooms and chard, leaving it to melt through the mixture.

Combine the kasha with the mushrooms, chard, herbs, and radishes. To serve, squeeze over the lemon juice, drizzle with olive oil, and season with a little salt and pepper.

BRUSSELS SPROUT CAESAR WITH CROUTONS, BORLOTTI BEANS, AND SUNFLOWER SEEDS

The Caesar salad is very much the perfect Italian–American invention. Nowadays, every self-respecting salad-maker needs to have a Caesar recipe in their repertoire. This one is mine. This Caesar shamelessly delivers flavor while also offering a nutritional punch—there are raw brussels sprouts from the antioxidant-rich brassica family, teamed with health-kicking borlotti beans, and vitamin E–packed sunflower seeds.

SERVES 4~6

½ lb (250 g) stale bread, torn into
   1 in (2 cm) chunks
1–2 tablespoons extra-virgin olive oil
1 lb (500 g) brussels sprouts, trimmed
One and one half 15 oz cans (500 g) borlotti
   beans (about 2 cups), drained
½ small red onion, very finely sliced
½ cup flat-leaf parsley leaves, chopped
½ cup basil leaves, roughly torn
½ cup sunflower seeds, toasted
¼ cup (60 g) parmesan, shaved
Sea salt and black pepper

CAESAR DRESSING

6 garlic cloves, unpeeled, plus ½ garlic
   clove, very finely chopped (optional)
1 cup (250 g) whole egg mayonnaise
⅓ cup (80 g) sour cream
1 tablespoon salted capers, rinsed
   and chopped
Juice of ½ lemon
Sea salt and black pepper

SUBSTITUTES

Brussels sprouts: kale
Borlotti beans: chickpeas, cannellini
   beans, or any other canned legume

Preheat the oven to 400°F (200°C).

Coat the bread in the olive oil and sprinkle with salt. Spread over a large baking tray in a single layer and bake in the oven until golden, about 15–20 minutes, turning every now and then to make sure the croutons are evenly browned and crisp on all sides. Cool.

While the croutons are baking, make the Caesar dressing. Place the unpeeled garlic cloves in the oven and cook for 20–25 minutes until they are very soft. Remove from the oven and peel off the skins, then mash the soft garlic flesh with the back of a fork and mix it together with the mayonnaise, sour cream, capers, lemon juice, and 3–4 teaspoons of water. Season to taste with salt and pepper and—if you like it more garlicky—add half a very finely chopped raw garlic clove.

Using a mandoline or the grater attachment on the food processor, very finely slice the brussels sprouts.

Combine the brussels sprouts with the borlotti beans, red onion, herbs, and half the sunflower seeds. Add the Caesar dressing, season with salt and pepper, and mix everything well to make sure the ingredients are well coated. Leave the salad to sit for 15–20 minutes to allow the brussels sprouts to soften and the flavors to meld together. To serve, fold through the croutons and sprinkle over the parmesan shavings and remaining sunflower seeds.

SUGAR SNAP PEAS WITH RADISH AND SPELT GRAINS

When I met natural foods chef, food writer, blogger, and native New Yorker Jodi Moreno, I knew I had found a friend. Jodi and I share a lot in common, including a love of vegetables and grains. One fine spring day, Jodi brought a bag of sugar snap peas to my Carroll Gardens apartment and prompted me to eat them raw, sliced in razor thin strips. What a revelation! This is the surprising, nourishing grain salad that I shared with Jodi, brought to life by these juicy, crunchy sugar snaps.

SERVES 4~6

2¼ cups (400 g) spelt grains
1 lb (400 g) sugar snap peas, trimmed
4 radishes (about 5 oz; 150 g), trimmed
4 green onions (see note page 32),
   finely chopped
½ cup cilantro leaves
2 tablespoons sesame seeds
Sea salt and black pepper

GINGER, HONEY, AND LEMON DRESSING

1 in (2.5 cm) piece of ginger, peeled and
   grated
1 small garlic clove, grated
Juice of 1 small lemon
2 tablespoons honey
1 tablespoon sesame oil
⅓ cup (80 ml) extra-virgin olive oil
Sea salt and black pepper

SUBSTITUTES/OPTIONS

Spelt: pearl barley, farro, freekeh
Sugar snap peas: snow peas, asparagus
For gluten free, use quinoa in place of spelt
For vegans, use maple syrup in place
   of honey

Add the spelt grains to a saucepan of salted water and bring to a boil. Reduce the heat and simmer, uncovered, for 30–35 minutes until the grains are tender. Drain.

To make the ginger, honey, and lemon dressing, combine all the ingredients in a small bowl and whisk together. Season well with salt and pepper.

Using a sharp knife, finely slice the sugar snap peas lengthways. Shave or slice the radishes into thin rounds. Place the sugar snap peas and radishes in a large serving bowl and add the green onion, cilantro leaves, and spelt grains. Add the dressing, season with salt and pepper, and toss to combine. To serve, scatter over the sesame seeds.

FREEKEH WITH DELI VEGETABLES, KALE PESTO, AND CHILI-PARMESAN SUNFLOWER SEEDS

This salad is an homage to all the multi-cultural delicatessens that are the heart of so many neighborhoods around the world. Invariably family run, the local "deli" is your go-to, where you can reliably find a great selection of cheeses, cold meats, pasta, olive oils, and marinated vegetables. This salad uses your favorite deli ingredients—try deliciously wilted Moroccan olives, perfectly acidic artichoke hearts, stunningly shriveled sun-dried tomatoes, smoky chargrilled eggplant or juicy salted capers. The addition of kale pesto and chili-parmesan sunflower seeds elevates this throw-together salad from simple to spectacular.

SERVES 4~6

4 cups marinated deli vegetables (about 4 lbs; 2 kg) such as sun-dried tomatoes, artichokes, olives, capers, eggplants, and bell peppers
2½ cups (400 g) freekeh, rinsed
3 tablespoons roughly chopped flat-leaf parsley leaves
½ cup basil leaves, torn
Juice of ½ lemon
Sea salt and black pepper

KALE PESTO

½ bunch of kale leaves, washed thoroughly
1 garlic clove, very finely chopped
½ cup sunflower seeds, toasted
¾ cup (185 ml) extra-virgin olive oil
3 tablespoons grated parmesan
Sea salt and black pepper

CHILI-PARMESAN SUNFLOWER SEEDS

¾ cup sunflower seeds
1 tablespoon extra-virgin olive oil
2 tablespoons grated parmesan
½ teaspoon chili powder or red pepper flakes

SUBSTITUTES/OPTIONS

Freekeh: spelt, farro, pearl barley
For gluten free, use quinoa in place of freekeh

Roughly chop or tear up the marinated vegetables with your hands. The shape and size is up to you.

Add the freekeh to a large saucepan of salted water and bring to a boil. Reduce the heat to a simmer and cook, uncovered, for 40–45 minutes until the grains are tender. Drain.

To make the pesto, blitz the kale, garlic, and sunflower seeds together in a food processor, gradually adding the olive oil along with 1 tablespoon of water, until you have a smooth, green sauce. Stir in the parmesan and season to taste with salt and pepper.

For the chili-parmesan sunflower seeds, preheat the oven to 300°F (150°C). In a bowl, combine the sunflower seeds, olive oil, parmesan, and chili powder or flakes (the heat factor is dependent upon the type of chili powder you use, so exercise your discretion here and vary the amount according to your preference). Mix well to coat the seeds evenly in the flavorings, spread on a baking tray and bake for 10–12 minutes until the cheese is melted and the seeds are golden.

Combine the freekeh, marinated vegetables, and herbs, and season with salt and pepper. Squeeze over the lemon juice, spoon over big dollops of the kale pesto, and fold through gently. To serve, sprinkle over some chili-parmesan sunflower seeds (you may have extra, so store them in an airtight jar to snack on later).

SO FRENCHIE

Recently, I left a little of my heart in France. I left it at the boulangerie where I picked up my daily bread (and perhaps snuck in a chocolate and banana croissant or two). I left it at the cafe where they serve bowls of creamy café au lait and the flakiest pastries for breakfast. I left it at the bistro where the chèvre chaud salad kept me coming back for more. I left it at the regional Provençal market where we decadently consumed locally grown autumnal produce and artisanal cheeses. I left it in the quiet town of waterways and cobblestone streets where we meandered aimlessly and happily. France is a revolutionary country in more ways than one, and in their food, they are still a nation that truly goes their own, delicious way.

CUMIN-SPICED CAULIFLOWER WITH FRIED LENTILS AND SPINACH YOGURT

I first cooked this salad in my (temporary) French kitchen in Isle sur la Sorgue, after a market visit left me with a plump cauliflower, a bag of puy lentils, and a crazy hankering for salad! Cumin adds a lovely mellow earthiness to the roasted cauli, while crispy fried lentils and a punchy spinach-laced yogurt bring a touch of celebration to this salad.

GF | SERVES 4~6

2 cauliflower heads (about 3½ lbs; 1.5 kg), cut into florets
1 tablespoon ground cumin
3–5 tablespoons extra-virgin olive oil
1½ cups (300 g) puy lentils, rinsed
1 bay leaf
1 garlic clove, very finely chopped
2 teaspoons ground coriander
1 teaspoon paprika
½ cup cilantro leaves, chopped
½ cup mint leaves
3 tablespoons roughly chopped toasted almonds (optional)
Sea salt and black pepper

SPINACH YOGURT

1 cup baby spinach leaves, washed thoroughly and finely chopped
1 tablespoon salted capers, rinsed and finely chopped
1½ cups (375 g) Greek yogurt
½ cup mint leaves, finely sliced
½ cup (100 ml) extra-virgin olive oil
Juice of ½ lemon
Sea salt and black pepper

Preheat the oven to 400°F (200°C).

Place the cauliflower on a large baking tray, sprinkle over the cumin, drizzle over 1–2 tablespoons of olive oil, and mix well. Season with salt and pepper and roast for 25–30 minutes until golden.

Meanwhile, bring a large saucepan of water to a boil, add the lentils and bay leaf, and cook for 20–25 minutes, until the lentils are just tender. Drain.

To make the spinach yogurt, whiz together the spinach, capers, yogurt, mint, and olive oil in a food processor. Squeeze over the lemon juice and season well with salt and pepper.

Heat 1 tablespoon of olive oil in a frying pan, add the garlic, coriander, paprika, and cooked lentils. Season well with salt and sauté over medium-high heat, shaking the pan to move the lentils around and adding another tablespoon of olive oil if needed, until the lentils are slightly crispy.

Spread the spinach yogurt out onto a large serving platter. Combine the roasted cauliflower with the fried lentils and herbs, drizzle with olive oil, and season well with salt and pepper. Spoon the cauliflower mixture over the yogurt and top with the almonds, if using.

PARSLEY, MACHE, AND COMTE PESTO WITH ROASTED BRUSSELS SPROUTS, GREEN BEANS, AND QUINOA

This salad celebrates the beautiful autumnal produce found at the local markets in Isle sur la Sorgue, just outside of Avignon, France. During this season, parsley is practically the only herb you see, mache (also known as lamb's lettuce or corn salad) is at its mellow best, and comte cheese (my all-time favorite breed of fromage) is in abundant supply. This all makes for a pretty delicious salad!

GF | SERVES 4~6

2¼ lbs (1 kg) brussels sprouts, trimmed and halved
2–3 tablespoons extra-virgin olive oil
1 cup (200 g) white or red quinoa (or a mixture), rinsed
1½ cups (375 ml) vegetable stock
½ lb (250 g) green beans, trimmed
½ cup pitted black olives, torn
½ cup flat-leaf parsley leaves, roughly chopped
Sea salt and black pepper

PARSLEY, MACHE, AND COMTE PESTO

1 small garlic clove, roughly chopped
¾ cup flat-leaf parsley leaves, roughly chopped
1 cup mache (lamb's lettuce)
1½ oz (40 g) almonds (or pine nuts), roughly chopped
½ cup (125 ml) extra-virgin olive oil
Zest and juice of ½ lemon
1½ oz (40 g) comte cheese, grated
Sea salt and black pepper

SUBSTITUTES

Comte: gruyere, cheddar
Mache (lamb's lettuce): baby arugula leaves, spinach leaves

Preheat the oven to 400°F (200°C).

To make the pesto, place the garlic in a mortar and sprinkle over a good pinch of salt. Pound with the pestle to form a paste, then add the parsley and mache and pound until the leaves have broken down. Add the nuts and pound again to a rough paste, then slowly pour over the oil and stir together until smooth. Add the lemon zest and juice and the cheese and season with salt and pepper to taste.

Place the brussels sprouts on a baking tray, drizzle with 1–2 tablespoons of oil, and season with salt and pepper. Roast for 20–25 minutes until tender and golden.

Add the quinoa and vegetable stock to a saucepan and bring to a gentle boil. Reduce the heat to low and leave to simmer for 15 minutes, or until the quinoa is tender and translucent and all the liquid has been absorbed (if there is any liquid left over at this point simply drain it off). Leave the quinoa in the hot saucepan off the heat for 5–10 minutes to allow it to dry out, then fluff up the grains with a fork.

In a frying pan, heat 1 tablespoon of olive oil and add the green beans with a pinch of salt. Sauté for 3–4 minutes, until the beans are just tender and starting to turn golden.

Combine the brussels sprouts, beans, quinoa, and olives. Spoon over the pesto and stir well, then scatter over the parsley to finish.

PROVENÇAL EGGPLANT WITH ROASTED RED PEPPERS, ZUCCHINI, GREEN BEANS, AND PUY LENTILS

Our recent time spent in France has really changed the way I view food. Most importantly, it has highlighted the joys of simple eating—spectacular meals made from humble ingredients. This salad was conceived during our visit to the Provençal neighborhood of Isle sur la Sorgue. Here, against the backdrop of charming waterways and picturesque autumnal sunsets, our twice-weekly ritual of visiting the local produce markets gave us incredible cooking inspiration. This salad is inspired by Provençal ratatouille and is enjoyed with French lentils, arugula, and salty, wilted black olives.

VG | GF | SERVES 4~6

8–9 tablespoons extra-virgin olive oil

2 large eggplants (about 2½ lbs; 1.1 kg), halved lengthways and sliced diagonally into ½ in (1 cm) pieces

2 zucchini (about 1 lb; 500 g), sliced diagonally into ½ in (1 cm) pieces

1 onion, finely sliced

1 garlic clove, very finely chopped

2 red bell peppers (about 1 lb; 450 g), deseeded and sliced into thin strips

4 roma tomatoes (about 1 lb; 500 g), roughly chopped

1 tablespoon red wine vinegar

2 teaspoons herbes de Provençe

½ lb (200 g) green beans, trimmed and halved

1½ lb (300 g) puy lentils, rinsed

½ cup pitted black olives (preferably wrinkly ones), torn in half

2 cups baby arugula leaves

½ cup flat-leaf parsley leaves, finely chopped

Sea salt and black pepper

SUBSTITUTES

Red bell peppers: store-bought roasted red peppers

Herbes de Provençe: dried basil, marjoram, rosemary, parsley, oregano, or thyme

Preheat the oven to 400°F (200°C).

Before roasting, I like to shallow-fry the eggplant and zucchini to soften them and start the process of caramelization. Heat 1–2 tablespoons of olive oil in a large frying pan. Add some of the eggplant slices in a single layer, sprinkle with a little salt, and pan-fry, turning often, until slightly softened and golden on both sides. Repeat, adding more olive oil between batches, until all the eggplant slices have been cooked, then repeat with the zucchini. Set aside.

In a large roasting pan, combine the onion, garlic, bell peppers, tomatoes, red wine vinegar, herbes de Provençe, and 4 tablespoons of olive oil. Season with salt and pepper and roast for 25 minutes until the tomatoes and peppers are soft. Remove the tomatoes and peppers from the pan, add the eggplant, zucchini, and green beans and roast for another 20–25 minutes, until all the vegetables are very tender. Season to taste.

Bring a large saucepan of water to a boil, add the lentils and a big pinch of salt, and simmer over medium heat for around 20 minutes or until the lentils are tender but still have a bite to them. Drain.

To serve, combine the roasted vegetables with the lentils, olives, arugula, and parsley. Season well and finish with a good drizzle of oil.

BASIL-OLIVE TAPENADE WITH POTATOES, PASTA, GREEN BEANS, AND CAPERS

This salad is perfect picnic or barbecue fare, marrying two outdoor dining staples—potato salad and pasta salad—into one very tasty offering. The delicious basil-scented olive tapenade is wonderful slathered on just cooked, still warm potatoes and pasta. This salad is on the starchy side, but it is extremely satisfying and you may find it popular with all of the family, even the young ones. Experiment with your favorite potato variety and pasta shape.

VG | SERVES 4~6

1½ lb (700 g) kipfler potatoes or other
    medium-sized waxy potatoes, halved
1 lb (500 g) short pasta (such as penne,
    orecchiette, or rigatoni)
2 tablespoons extra-virgin olive oil
½ lb (200 g) green beans, trimmed and
    halved
3 tablespoons sunflower seeds, toasted
¼ cup (60 g) salted capers, rinsed
½ cup flat-leaf parsley leaves, finely chopped
Sea salt

BASIL-OLIVE TAPENADE

2 garlic cloves
1 cup basil leaves
½ cup pitted black olives
    (preferably wrinkly ones)
½ cup walnuts, toasted
⅓ cup (80 ml) extra-virgin olive oil
1 teaspoon white wine vinegar
Sea salt and black pepper

SUBSTITUTES

Kipfler potatoes: sweet potato,
    Jerusalem artichokes
Green beans: asparagus, garden peas

To make the tapenade, place the garlic in a mortar, sprinkle over a pinch of salt, and pound with a pestle to form a paste. Add the basil and pound until the leaves have broken down, then add the olives and walnuts and pound again until you get a thick paste. Stir in the olive oil and vinegar and season with pepper. (Alternatively, you can always throw these ingredients in a food processor and blitz away.)

Bring a large saucepan of salted water to a boil, add the potatoes, and cook for 15–20 minutes until they are just tender—the exact cooking time will depend on the size and variety of your potatoes so keep an eye on them, as you don't want them so soft that they are breaking apart. When ready, drain.

Bring another saucepan of salted water to a boil. Add the pasta and cook according to the packet instructions until al dente. Drain and combine the warm pasta with the warm potatoes.

Heat 1 tablespoon of olive oil in a frying pan, add the green beans and sauté for 4–5 minutes until the beans are bright green, just tender, and beginning to color.

Combine the tapenade, pasta, potatoes, and beans along with a swirl of olive oil to loosen everything up. Toss together well. To serve, scatter over the sunflower seeds, capers, and parsley.

SMASHED EGGPLANT WITH LENTILS AND MAPLE-ROASTED RADISH

While in Provence, I heard about a regally monikered local dish called "eggplant caviar" that immediately sparked my interest. While it is actually just a simple eggplant dip, this dish encapsulates the respect shown to fresh produce in regional French cuisine. My take on eggplant caviar is lighter than baba ghanoush and is a lovely accompaniment to these rather spectacular roasted radishes. Sneak some of the smashed eggplant aside to use as a dip!

VG | GF | SERVES 4~6

2 cups (400 g) lentils (any variety), rinsed
1 bay leaf
1 small garlic clove, peeled (optional)
30 radishes (about 2 lb; 1 kg), trimmed
    and quartered
1 tablespoon maple syrup
Juice of 1 lemon
2 cups baby spinach leaves
½ cup flat-leaf parsley leaves
2 tablespoons extra-virgin olive oil
Sea salt and black pepper

SMASHED EGGPLANT

3 eggplants (about 2½ lb; 1.2 kg)
½ cup (125 ml) extra-virgin olive oil
1 small garlic clove, grated
Juice of 1 lemon, plus extra if necessary
1 shallot (see note page 32), finely diced
½ teaspoon paprika
½ teaspoon chili powder
2 tablespoons finely chopped flat-leaf
    parsley leaves
2 tablespoons finely chopped mint leaves
Sea salt and black pepper

SUBSTITUTES

Maple syrup: honey, agave syrup

To make the smashed eggplant, place the eggplants directly on the flame of a gas stovetop, over a very hot barbecue, or in an oven preheated to 425°F (220°C). Cook, turning often, until they become very soft and the skin is charred all over (this process takes a while, especially when using an open flame, so be patient!). When cool enough to handle, carefully peel the charred skin off the eggplants. Place the eggplant flesh in a large bowl and break it up with a fork. Add the olive oil, garlic, lemon juice, shallot, paprika, chili powder, and a large pinch of salt, and mash everything together, then stir in the parsley and mint. Taste and add more lemon or salt as necessary (the eggplant needs liberal seasoning, so don't be afraid of adding more salt if needed). Alternatively, place everything in the bowl of a food processor and whiz it together.

Bring a large pot of water to a boil, add the lentils, bay leaf, whole garlic clove, if using, and a big pinch of salt, and cook for 20–25 minutes until just tender. Drain.

Place the radishes on a large baking tray and drizzle over the maple syrup and half the lemon juice. Toss to combine and roast in the oven for 20–25 minutes until the radishes are tender.

Combine the radishes with the lentils, spinach leaves, parsley, olive oil, and the remaining lemon juice and season with salt and pepper. To serve, spread the smashed eggplant over a large serving dish and top with the radishes and lentils.

KINDA-NIÇOISE WITH FRIED GREEN BEANS, ROASTED KALE, LENTILS, STEAMED EGGS, AND CAPER MAYO

There is much to love about a classic salade niçoise. As with many rustic French salads, niçoise tradition-ally brims with the freshest local produce—olives, oil-cured tuna, anchovies, and tender green beans. My version celebrates the traditional salty, acidic, green-ness of a classic niçoise, bringing in unbelievably soft, silky steamed eggs as my protein component. Steaming eggs is a nifty little trick I learned from my friend Elham Abi-Ghanem, the best egg cook I know!

GF | SERVES 4~6

6 large eggs, at room temperature
1 cup (200 g) puy lentils, rinsed
2–3 tablespoons extra-virgin olive oil
⅓ lb (150 g) green beans, trimmed and
    halved
1 bunch of kale leaves, washed thoroughly,
    central stems removed, leaves torn
½ cup basil leaves, torn
½ cup flat-leaf parsley leaves
1 tablespoon tarragon leaves
½ small red onion, very finely sliced
3 radishes (about ¼ lb; 100 g), very finely
    sliced
½ lb (200 g) cherry tomatoes, halved
½ cup pitted black olives (any variety), torn
2 teaspoons red wine vinegar
Sea salt and black pepper

CAPER MAYONNAISE

1 cup (250 g) whole-egg mayonnaise
½ cup (125 g) natural yogurt
1 tablespoon extra-virgin olive oil
1 tablespoon salted capers, rinsed and
    roughly chopped
Squeeze of lemon juice
1 small garlic clove, very finely chopped
Sea salt and black pepper

SUBSTITUTE

Puy lentils: another variety of lentil

To make the caper mayonnaise, whisk together the mayonnaise, yogurt, and olive oil until well combined. Stir in the capers, lemon juice, and garlic, and season with pepper and a little salt to taste (you shouldn't need much salt as the capers will already make this quite salty).

Fill a saucepan with water to a depth of 1 in (3 cm) and sit a steamer basket on the top. Place the eggs in the steamer basket, cover with a lid, and bring the water to a boil. Steam the eggs for around 5 minutes for soft-boiled, 7 minutes for medium, or around 9 minutes for hard-boiled. (Of course, the amount of time will depend on the size of your eggs, so you may have to try this a few times to get it perfect for you!) When ready, immediately cool under cold running water.

Add the lentils to a saucepan of salted water, bring to a boil, and cook for 20–25 minutes until just tender. Drain.

In a large frying pan, add 1 tablespoon of olive oil and fry the green beans for 3–4 minutes until they are just tender and are starting to char. Remove the beans from the pan and add another tablespoon of oil, then add the kale and cook for a few minutes until wilted and starting to color.

Combine the beans, kale, and herbs with the red onion, radishes, tomatoes, olives, and lentils. Pour over the red wine vinegar, drizzle with some olive oil, and season with salt and pepper. To serve, pile the salad on a serving dish and drizzle the caper mayo over the top. Peel the eggs, then break up or slice them and place over the salad, finishing with a few good grinds of pepper.

PROVENÇAL GRAIN SALAD WITH GREEN BEANS
AND LEMON-PARSLEY OIL

This is a salad I cooked regularly during our stay in Provence, using locally grown red rice from Camargue. This hearty grain salad can be enjoyed warm during the cooler months, but is also lovely served at room temperature for warm summer days. The lemon-parsley oil provides a beautiful citrus lift to the dish. Use other herbs for the oil if you wish—basil, oregano, tarragon, or chives also work well.

VG | SERVES 4~6

½ cup (100 g) Camargue red rice
1 cup (200 g) brown rice
½ cup (100 g) quinoa (white, red, or a mix), rinsed
½ cup (100 g) coarse bulgur wheat (cracked wheat)
1 tablespoon extra-virgin olive oil
½ lb (200 g) green beans, trimmed and cut into 1 in (2 cm) pieces
One half 15 oz can (250 g) chickpeas (about 1 cup), drained and rinsed
12 pitted green olives
3 tablespoons finely sliced green onions (see note page 32)
½ cup flat-leaf parsley leaves, finely chopped
3 tablespoons walnuts, toasted and crushed
Sea salt and black pepper

LEMON-PARSLEY OIL

1 small garlic clove, very finely chopped
½ cup flat-leaf parsley leaves, chopped
3 tablespoons extra-virgin olive oil
1 tablespoon walnut oil (or other neutral oil like grapeseed)
Squeeze of lemon juice
Sea salt and black pepper

SUBSTITUTES

Camargue red rice: wild rice, black rice

Add the red and brown rice to a saucepan with 6 cups (1.5 liters) of water and a big pinch of salt. Cover with a lid and bring to a boil over a medium-high heat, then reduce the heat to a simmer and leave to cook for 15–20 minutes, until the grains are soft and all the water has been absorbed (if there is any water left at this point, simply drain it away). If you prefer, you can cook this in a rice cooker instead.

Combine the quinoa and bulgur wheat and cook them in 2 cups (500 ml) of salted water until soft, draining off any remaining water as before. Leave the mixture to sit in the hot saucepan for 5–10 minutes to dry out and fluff up.

Heat the olive oil in a small frying pan over a high heat, add the beans, and fry with a pinch of salt for 4–5 minutes until tender and starting to brown. Leave to cool.

To make the lemon-parsley oil, add the garlic and 1 teaspoon of salt to a mortar and pound together with a pestle to form a rough paste. Add the parsley and pound until the leaves are broken down and the paste is green, then stir in the oils and lemon juice, and season to taste with salt and pepper.

Combine the red rice, brown rice, quinoa, bulgur wheat, chickpeas, green beans, green olives, green onion, and parsley in a big bowl and stir well, then season with salt and pepper. To serve, scatter over the walnuts and drizzle over the lemon-parsley oil.

ROASTED CHESTNUTS WITH PAN-FRIED PEARS, BLUE CHEESE, BELGIAN ENDIVE, AND MUSTARD VINAIGRETTE

Provincial markets are the lifeblood of big and small towns all over France, and are vital in providing locals with their daily necessities. There are no fancy food purveyors here, this is real food—grown, made and baked locally. In the autumn, markets in Provence are abundant with chestnuts, pears, and Belgian endive, so this is my version of a French market salad. The chestnuts take a little time to prepare, but while they are roasting they will fill your house with the sweetest aroma that makes it totally worth the effort.

GF | SERVES 4~6

1 lb (500 g) chestnuts
1½ tablespoons (20 g) salted butter
1 tablespoon honey
3 thyme sprigs
5 beurre bosc pears (about 2½ lb; 1.1 kg),
   cores removed, peeled and each
   cut into 8 wedges
1 head butter lettuce, leaves picked apart
2 Belgian endive, leaves picked apart and
   torn
3 tablespoons finely chopped chives
3 tablespoons finely chopped flat-leaf
   parsley leaves
7 oz (200 g) soft blue cheese, crumbled
¼ cup hazelnuts, toasted, skinned
   and roughly chopped
Sea salt and black pepper

MUSTARD VINAIGRETTE

1 tablespoon dijon mustard
2 tablespoons cider vinegar
2 tablespoons honey
⅓ cup (80 ml) extra-virgin olive oil
1 garlic clove, very finely chopped
Sea salt and black pepper

Preheat the oven to 350°F (180°C).

Prepare the chestnuts by scoring them with a sharp knife, working your way around their circumference and being careful not to cut too deep into the flesh. (Scoring the chestnuts like this helps the skin to come off once they are cooked.)

Place the scored chestnuts on a large baking tray and roast in the oven for 25–30 minutes, until the tough outer skins have cracked open and the insides are tender. While they are still hot, peel away the outer skins and the papery skins inside.

Melt the butter together with the honey and thyme sprigs in a large frying pan. Add the pears and cook gently for 5 minutes, turning, until softened and starting to brown.

To make the mustard vinaigrette, whisk together all the ingredients and season with salt and pepper.

Combine the butter lettuce and endive leaves with the chestnuts, chives, and parsley. Add the vinaigrette, season lightly with salt and pepper, and toss together. Arrange the salad on a large serving platter and top with the pears and the cooking syrup from the pan. Dot with the crumbled blue cheese and scatter over the chopped hazelnuts to finish.

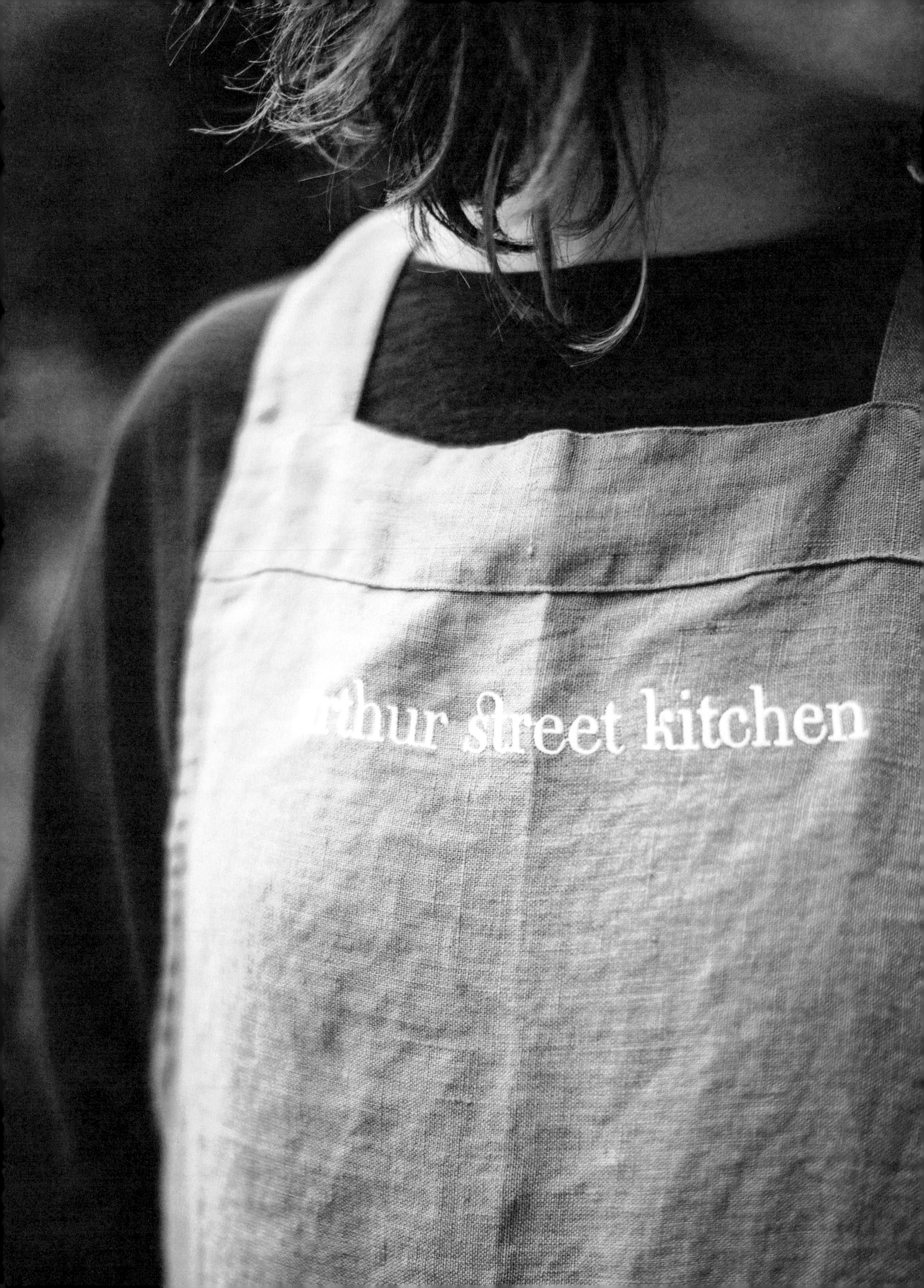
street kitchen

WARM GOAT'S CHEESE CROUTONS WITH ROASTED BEETS, FIGS, AND APPLE-MUSTARD DRESSING

A trip to Paris invariably means high salade au chèvre chaud consumption, which is fine by me! In a city where vegetarian food can still be hard to come by, this hot goat's cheese salad has saved me too many times to recall. This is such a beautifully simple salad with the most harmonious flavors. My version includes roasted beets, figs, and a divine apple-mustard dressing. Use whatever salad leaves you have on hand for this.

SERVES 4~6

6 small beets (about 1¾ lb; 800 g), peeled and cut into small wedges
2 tablespoons extra-virgin olive oil
⅓ lb (150 g) baguette, sliced into 1 in (2 cm) thick rounds
7 oz (200 g) goat's cheese log, rind on
5 thyme sprigs, leaves picked
2 teaspoons chopped rosemary leaves
3 cups watercress
3 cups mache (lamb's lettuce)
3 tablespoons chopped chives
4 figs, each cut into 8 segments
1 cup walnuts, toasted and crushed
Sea salt and black pepper

APPLE-MUSTARD DRESSING

3 tablespoons apple juice
2 tablespoons extra-virgin olive oil
1 tablespoon honey
1 tablespoon dijon mustard
1 tablespoon cider vinegar
1 small garlic clove, very finely chopped
Sea salt and black pepper

SUBSTITUTES

Mache (lamb's lettuce): baby spinach leaves
Watercress: baby arugula leaves

Preheat the oven to 400°F (200°C).

Spread the beets on a large baking tray, drizzle with 1 tablespoon of olive oil, season with salt and pepper, and roast for 30–35 minutes until tender.

Preheat the grill to high. Place the baguette slices on a baking tray, drizzle over 1 tablespoon of olive oil, and place under the hot grill for 2 minutes, or until golden. Remove the croutons from the grill.

Slice the goat's cheese into as many rounds as you have croutons. Place a slice of cheese on the un-grilled side of each crouton and top with a few thyme and rosemary leaves. Return to the grill and cook for 3–4 minutes, or until the goat's cheese is soft and golden.

To make the dressing, whisk together all the ingredients and season with salt and pepper to taste.

Toss the salad leaves together with the chives. To serve, arrange the beet slices and figs on top of the leaves, drizzle over the apple-mustard dressing and season with salt and pepper. Top with the goat's cheese croutons and the walnuts.

GLOBE ARTICHOKES WITH CANNELLINI BEANS, CHERRY TOMATOES, LEMON, AND BUFFALO MOZZARELLA

For years, I resisted the urge to cook globe artichokes. Their natural thistled beauty fascinated me, but, to be honest, I wondered if all that preparation was really worth it. But while in Provence, with time and patience on our side and armed with beautiful globes from the local market, our family finally discovered the joys of freshly prepared artichokes. And yes, they are most definitely worth the effort. Try this once and you'll be hooked (though if you can't be bothered, store-bought marinated artichokes hearts are fine too!).

SERVES 4~6

Zest and juice of 1 lemon
6 globe artichokes (about 3 lb; 1.3 kg)
2¼ cups (400 g) spelt grains
2–3 tablespoons extra-virgin olive oil
1 garlic clove, very finely chopped
1 tablespoon finely chopped rosemary leaves
2 teaspoons finely chopped oregano leaves
½ lb (250 g) cherry tomatoes, halved
One and one half 15 oz cans (500 g)
    cannellini beans (about 2 cups), drained
2 cups baby arugula leaves
10 oz (300 g) buffalo mozzarella, torn into
    chunks
1 long red chili, deseeded and sliced into
    very thin strips
½ cup basil leaves, torn
3 tablespoons pine nuts, toasted
Sea salt and black pepper

Begin by preparing the artichokes. Squeeze half the lemon juice into a large bowl of water. Trim the artichoke stalks to about 1½ in (3 cm) in length, then slice about 1 in (2 cm) off the top of each globe. Peel away and discard the outer two or three layers of the artichoke until you get to the inner yellow leaves, then trim around the stalk with a paring knife, peeling away the tough outer skin. Cut the artichokes in half, carefully remove and discard the furry chokes, and place the artichoke halves in the bowl of lemon water to stop them from browning.

Bring a pot of salted water to a boil. Add the spelt grains and cook for 20–25 minutes until tender. Drain.

Slice the prepared artichoke halves into thin wedges. Heat 1–2 tablespoons of olive oil in a large frying pan over medium-high heat, add the garlic, rosemary, and oregano leaves and cook until fragrant, about 30 seconds. Add the artichoke pieces along with a big pinch of salt and pepper and sauté for 4–5 minutes, adding a splash of water halfway through cooking, until tender.

Combine the tomatoes, cannellini beans, spelt grains, and arugula leaves, and spread the mixture evenly over a large serving plate or platter. Dot the artichokes, mozzarella, chili strips, and torn basil over the salad, then add the lemon zest and the remaining lemon juice. To serve, season well with sea salt and black pepper, drizzle with olive oil, and scatter over the pine nuts.

INTO THE
MEDITERRANEAN

*Into the Mediterranean we go,
alive with blue skies, pebble shores,
cerulean seas, bucolic settings, and
sun-blistered skin. Memories of
vacations among the flaxen hillsides
and soaring mountains of bountiful
Italy and Spain, rapaciously
feeding upon the Mediterranean
diet of plump tomatoes, creamy
cheeses, fresh pasta, bright herbs,
perky citrus, and sharp acids. Salty
olives and capers enliven nourishing
grains and legumes. Crusty bread
a must at every meal. Each and
every dish completed by lashings of
earthy olive oil. The Mediterranean
way to eat is perfectly simple and
simply perfect.*

CHARGRILLED BROCCOLI, ZUCCHINI, PEAS, AND RADISH WITH CANNELLINI BEANS AND CAPER BAGNA CAUDA

This salad is as green as they come, brimming with the vitality and color of summer's most abundant vegetables. It features my take on Italian bagna cauda, a traditional Piedmontese dip using capers in place of anchovies. I like my bagna cauda very lemony, but vary the amount of juice according to your desires. Serve with some crusty Italian bread to mop up the salty, lemony goodness.

SERVES 4~6

2 small broccoli heads (about 1¾ lb; 800 g),
    cut into florets
3 zucchini, sliced diagonally into
    ¼ in (5 mm) pieces
2–3 tablespoons extra-virgin olive oil
⅓ lb (150 g) garden peas (fresh or frozen)
One and one half 15 oz cans (500 g)
    cannellini beans (about 2 cups), drained
2 radishes, shaved
½ cup basil leaves, torn
½ cup mint leaves, torn
½ cup flat-leaf parsley leaves, chopped
1 crusty Italian bread loaf, to serve
    (optional)
Sea salt and black pepper

CAPER BAGNA CAUDA

3 garlic cloves
⅓ cup (80 g) salted capers, rinsed
½ cup (125 ml) extra-virgin olive oil
7 tablespoons (100 g) salted butter
Zest and juice of 1 lemon

OPTION
For vegans, use olive oil in place of butter

Start by making the caper bagna cauda. Place the garlic cloves and capers in a large mortar and pound with a pestle until you have a chunky paste. Add the caper-garlic paste to a small frying pan along with the olive oil and butter, bring it to a simmer, and gently cook for a further 3–4 minutes. Remove from the heat and add the lemon zest and juice, adjusting the amount of citrus according to your personal preference. Keep warm.

Heat a griddle pan or barbecue to high. Coat the broccoli and zucchini in the olive oil and season with a big pinch of salt. Add the broccoli and zucchini to the pan or barbecue and cook, turning occasionally, until tender and slightly charred on all sides.

Bring a small pot of salted water to a boil, add the peas and blanch until just tender, about 1–2 minutes. Drain and refresh under cold running water.

Combine the broccoli, zucchini, peas, cannellini beans, and shaved radishes in a large bowl. Add the herbs and big sprinkle of salt and pepper and toss everything together well. Spoon the warm caper bagna cauda over the top and serve with crusty Italian bread, if you like.

CAPONATA WITH PEARL COUSCOUS AND ALMONDS

During our London years, my husband and I were devout Italophiles, visiting Italy often. One of our favorite places was Sicily. Here, we ate well and cheaply at tucked-away restaurants in Palermo and in the small fishing village called Sciacca, where we would feast on wonderful things like caponata. My take on this Sicilian classic is given a kick with the addition of harissa and is intensely sweet and sour. Feel free to adjust the amount of vinegar and sugar to your liking and taste.

VG | SERVES 4~6

3 small eggplants (about 1¾ lb; 800 g)

3–4 tablespoons extra-virgin olive oil

3–4 tablespoons sunflower oil

2 red bell peppers, deseeded and cut into
    1 in (2 cm) pieces

3 celery stalks, trimmed and finely sliced

2 onions, finely sliced

1 tablespoon harissa paste (store-bought
    or see my recipe on page 121)

One 15 oz can (400 g) diced tomatoes
    (about 1 cup)

2–3 tablespoons red wine vinegar

2 tablespoons salted capers, rinsed

½ cup pitted green Sicilian olives

2–3 teaspoons superfine sugar

Juice of ½ lemon

3 cups (500 g) pearl couscous

½ cup flat-leaf parsley leaves, finely chopped

½ cup slivered almonds, toasted

Sea salt and black pepper

OPTION

For gluten free, use quinoa or brown rice
    in place of couscous

Peel strips of skin from the eggplants, from top to bottom, so it leaves a stripy pattern. Cut the eggplants into 1 in (2 cm) cubes.

Heat 2 tablespoons each of the olive and sunflower oils in a large casserole dish. Add the eggplant and fry for 3–4 minutes over medium heat, turning often, until golden (you may have to do this in several batches to avoid overcrowding). Remove the eggplant from the dish and place in a colander. Sprinkle over some salt.

Add the bell peppers and celery to the casserole dish along with an extra tablespoon of sunflower oil if needed, and fry for 3 minutes until slightly softened. Season with a pinch of salt, then transfer to the colander with the eggplant.

Heat 1 tablespoon of olive oil in the casserole dish and add the onions. Cook for 2 minutes, then stir in the harissa paste and cook for another 5 minutes, or until the onions are soft. Return the eggplant, celery, and peppers to the pan and add the tomatoes, red wine vinegar, capers, and olives. Stir in the sugar and season with salt and pepper. If the mixture is a bit dry, add a few tablespoons of water (though just a little at a time, as the mixture will become more liquid as the vegetables cook). Cover and cook for 20 minutes over a low-medium heat, or until the vegetables are soft. When cooked, squeeze in some lemon juice and taste, seasoning again with salt and pepper if required.

Bring a large pot of salted water to a boil. Add the pearl couscous and cook for 8–10 minutes or until the couscous is tender. Drain and then add the vegetables.

In a large mixing bowl, spoon the caponata over the couscous and fold together so that the vegetables and sauce coat the balls of couscous. Finish with a drizzle of olive oil and sprinkle over the parsley and almonds.

WINTER PANZANELLA WITH ROASTED TOMATOES, FENNEL, KALE, AND CARAMELIZED BALSAMIC

Apart from being incredibly delicious, I love the practicality of a bread salad. It is the perfect way to use up all those leftover ends of bread loaves. The stars of a classic panzanella are the ripe, juicy tomatoes and the bread. The bread you choose is important—it needs to have a hearty texture with a crunchy crust, so I favor sourdough for this salad. This is a darker, deeper version of panzanella, heavier with vegetables, and finished with a super-simple-to-make caramelized balsamic vinegar. If you don't have fennel and kale on hand, you could also use other vegetables such as cucumber, zucchini, or radish.

VG | SERVES 4~6

1 lb (400 g) stale sourdough bread, torn into chunks

5 tablespoons (100 ml) extra-virgin olive oil

5 roma tomatoes (or any variety)

½ red onion, very finely sliced

4 thyme sprigs, leaves picked

½ teaspoon superfine sugar

3 fennel bulbs (about 2½ lb; 1.2 kg), cut into thick wedges

1 garlic clove, very finely chopped

½ bunch of kale leaves, washed thoroughly, central stems removed, leaves torn

3 tablespoons roughly chopped flat-leaf parsley leaves

½ cup basil leaves, torn

1 tablespoon oregano leaves

⅓ cup (80 ml) Caramelized Balsamic Vinegar (see below)

Sea salt and black pepper

CARAMELIZED BALSAMIC VINEGAR (MAKES ⅔ CUP/175 ML)

1 cup (250 ml) balsamic vinegar

2 tablespoons soft brown sugar

3 tablespoons superfine sugar, plus extra if necessary

Preheat the oven to 400°F (200°C).

To make the caramelized balsamic, add the vinegar and sugars to a small saucepan and heat gently until the sugars have dissolved. Increase the heat to high, bring to a boil, and cook for 5–10 minutes until the mixture has thickened and reduced by about half. Test it by placing a small amount on a cold spoon—it should look darker and run on the spoon less easily. This is a good opportunity to test it for sweetness, adding more superfine sugar if you desire. It will thicken further upon cooling.

Place the bread chunks on a large baking tray, drizzle over 2 tablespoons of olive oil, and sprinkle over a pinch of salt. Bake for 15 minutes, tossing halfway through, until the bread is golden and crispy on all sides.

Cut the tomatoes into chunks about 1 in (2 cm) in size. Place them in a bowl with the red onion, thyme leaves, 1 tablespoon of olive oil, and the sugar. Mix everything together well and season with salt and pepper. Set aside.

Spread the fennel over a large baking tray. Drizzle over 1 tablespoon of olive oil, season with salt and pepper, and roast for 20 minutes or until starting to turn golden. Spread the tomato and red onion mixture over the fennel pieces and roast for another 10–15 minutes until the tomatoes are softened and almost ready to collapse.

Heat 1 tablespoon of olive oil in a frying pan, add the garlic, kale, and a small pinch of salt and cook for 4–5 minutes until the kale leaves are wilted and starting to turn golden and crispy.

Combine the roasted vegetables with the croutons, kale, and herbs, and season with salt and pepper. Drizzle over the caramelized balsamic and toss together. Let the salad sit for 20–30 minutes or so to allow the flavors to soak into the bread, or eat straight away if you can't resist!

ROASTED RED PEPPERS AND CHERRY TOMATOES WITH PEARL BARLEY, CUMIN, AND SHERRY VINEGAR

Roasting dramatically intensifies the character of bell peppers, bringing out their natural sweetness and piquancy. Here, the natural roasting juices of the peppers, tomatoes, and onions cleverly morph into the salad dressing. This dish was inspired by one of my dearest friends, Davida Sweeney, who often extolls the delights of roasted red peppers drenched in olive oil and sherry vinegar, as is served in her native Spain.

SERVES 4~6

12 red bell peppers (about 5¼ lb; 2.4 kg), halved and deseeded
2 onions, each cut into 8 wedges
4 garlic cloves, unpeeled
4–5 tablespoons extra-virgin olive oil
1 lb (400 g) cherry tomatoes, halved
2 cups (400 g) pearl barley, rinsed
3 tablespoons roughly chopped flat-leaf parsley leaves
1 teaspoon superfine sugar
2 tablespoons sherry vinegar
1 teaspoon ground cumin
½ cup almonds, toasted and roughly chopped
3 oz (80 g) manchego cheese, shaved
Sea salt and black pepper

SUBSTITUTES

Red bell peppers: yellow or orange peppers
Manchego cheese: parmesan or pecorino

Preheat the oven to 400°F (200°C).

Arrange the bell pepper halves, cut-side down, in two large roasting pans along with the onion wedges and garlic cloves. Drizzle over 2–3 tablespoons of olive oil and season with salt and pepper. Roast for 35–40 minutes, adding the cherry tomatoes to the roasting pans 20 minutes into cooking, until the peppers are well softened. Remove from the oven and leave to cool.

When cool enough to handle, carefully peel the skin off the peppers and slice them into strips. Return to the pans with the roasted tomatoes and onions, squeezing the soft garlic flesh out of the skins and mashing it gently into the cooking juices with the back of a fork. Stir to combine.

Add the pearl barley and a big pinch of salt to a large saucepan. Bring to a boil and cook for 25–30 minutes until the barley is swollen and tender. Drain.

While the barley is still warm, add it to the pan with the peppers, tomatoes, and onions and stir to coat the barley in the "dressing." Add the parsley, sugar, sherry vinegar, and cumin, and drizzle with the remaining olive oil. Season with salt and pepper and gently mix together. To serve, sprinkle over the almonds and shaved manchego cheese.

PASTA E FAGIOLI WITH FENNEL AND CONFIT TOMATOES

One of my favorite things to do in the kitchen is to take a simple, classic concept and turn it into something a little bit special. This salad is a pretty fine example of turning rustic into remarkable, with pantry staples of pasta and beans given a sophisticated lift with dazzling confit tomatoes and crisp shaved fennel. The tomato cooking oil cleverly becomes a rather smashing scented oil to dress the salad. The confit tomatoes can be made a day ahead and stored in the refrigerator—just bring them to room temperature before adding to the salad.

VG | SERVES 4~6

½ lb (250 g) short pasta (such as orecchiette, rigatoni, penne, or cavatelli)
2 fennel bulbs (about 1¾; 800 g), finely shaved
One and one half 15 oz cans (500 g) borlotti beans (about 2 cups)
½ cup basil leaves, torn
3 tablespoons finely chopped flat-leaf parsley leaves
3 tablespoons roughly chopped oregano leaves
3 tablespoons pine nuts, toasted
Sea salt and black pepper

CONFIT TOMATOES

8 roma tomatoes (about 2¼ lb; 1 kg), quartered with seeds and membranes removed
5 thyme sprigs
1 bay leaf
3 garlic cloves, unpeeled
1 teaspoon sea salt
½ cup (125 ml) extra-virgin olive oil

Preheat the oven to 300°F (150°C).

For the confit tomatoes, choose a baking dish that will fit the tomatoes snugly. Arrange the tomatoes in the dish, scatter over the thyme sprigs, bay leaf, and garlic, sprinkle over the salt and pour over the olive oil. Roast for 1 hour 40 minutes, turning the tomatoes over 40 minutes into cooking, until the tomatoes are slightly shrunken but still plump. (The trick is to keep the temperature very low.) Leave the tomatoes to cool completely, reserving the cooking oil, then carefully peel off the skins.

Cook the pasta in a saucepan of boiling salted water, according to packet instructions, until al dente. Drain and refresh under cold, running water.

To serve, combine the pasta, fennel, borlotti beans, and herbs, and season with salt and pepper. Spoon over the confit tomatoes, pour over the confit cooking oil to flavor the salad, and top with the pine nuts.

SLOW-COOKED CHICKPEAS WITH ROASTED CARROTS, SPINACH, AND ZA'ATAR

There is a certain quiet elegance to this Mediterranean-inspired dish of slow-cooked chickpeas, patiently roasted in a flavorsome bell pepper and tomato puree with colorful spices. The joy in this dish is taking a simple pantry item—canned chickpeas—and turning it into something utterly spectacular.

VG | GF | SERVES 4~6

2 cups (500 g) tomato passata
1 teaspoon superfine sugar
Two 15 oz cans (750 g) chickpeas
   (about 3 cups), drained
10 small carrots (about 1¾; 800 g), peeled
1–2 tablespoons extra-virgin olive oil
3 cups baby spinach leaves,
   washed thoroughly
½ cup flat-leaf parsley leaves,
   roughly chopped
½ cup mint leaves
1 tablespoon za'atar
Sea salt and black pepper

RED PEPPER PASTE

⅓ cup (80 ml) extra-virgin olive oil
1 red onion, roughly chopped
2 garlic cloves, crushed
1 tablespoon tomato paste
1 teaspoon cayenne pepper
½ teaspoon smoked paprika
2 red bell peppers, deseeded and
   roughly diced
1 teaspoon sea salt

Preheat the oven to 400°F (200°C).

To make the red pepper paste, put all the ingredients in a food processor and blitz.

In a large pan, add the red pepper paste and fry over a medium heat, stirring occasionally, for 5 minutes. Add the tomato passata, sugar, chickpeas, and 1 cup (250 ml) of water. Bring to a very gentle simmer, cover and cook over a very low heat for 1 hour, stirring from time to time, and adding water as needed to maintain a sauce-like consistency (the sauce needs to thicken without the chickpeas becoming dry). When ready, leave to cool.

Place the carrots on a large baking tray, drizzle with the olive oil, and season well with salt and pepper. Roast for about 40 minutes until the carrots are tender and starting to turn golden.

To serve, spoon the chickpeas onto a large serving dish, scatter over the baby spinach, and arrange the carrots on top. To finish, sprinkle over the herbs and za'atar.

BLACKENED CHILI WITH BUFFALO MOZZARELLA, CANNELLINI BEANS, AND LEMON CRÈME FRAÎCHE

With this salad, I wanted to show the true flavor characteristics of chili, without diffusing the heat. When charred, chili exudes a sweet tang, reminiscent of roasted red peppers. The creamy buffalo mozzarella and smooth lemony crème fraîche harmoniously counterbalance the chili's feistiness, but you can use any fresh white cheese such as bocconcini, fior di latte, burrata, or even chunks of ricotta. Make sure you consume this salad (as almost always with salads) at room temperature!

GF | SERVES 4~6

5 long red chilies
2 cups baby arugula leaves
1 lb (500 g) buffalo mozzarella
4 roma tomatoes (about 1 lb; 500 g), finely sliced into rounds
One and one half 15 oz cans (500 g) cannellini beans (about 2 cups), drained
½ cup basil leaves, roughly torn
½ cup salted capers, rinsed
1–2 tablespoons extra-virgin olive oil
Juice of ½ lemon
Sea salt and black pepper

LEMON CRÈME FRAÎCHE

½ cup (100 g) crème fraîche
Zest and juice of ½ lemon, plus extra juice if necessary
1 tablespoon extra-virgin olive oil
Sea salt and black pepper

SUBSTITUTES

Chilies: red or yellow bell peppers
Buffalo mozzarella: bocconcini, fior di latte, burrata, ricotta

Start by blackening the chilies. I do this directly on the naked flame of a gas stovetop, but you can also place it under a hot grill or on a barbecue. Whichever cooking method you choose, you need to char the skin of the chili until it's all black and the flesh has softened. Turn the chilies often as the skin will blacken quite quickly. Leave to cool.

When cool enough to handle, wearing gloves, gently rub the blackened skin off the chilies under running water and dry with a paper towel. Cut each chili in half and carefully scrape away and discard the seeds and membrane. Cut the chili flesh into thin strips.

To make the lemon crème fraîche, stir the crème fraîche, lemon zest and juice, and the olive oil together. Season to taste with salt and pepper and adjust the lemon juice according to your preference.

Scatter the arugula leaves over a large serving plate. Slice or tear the buffalo mozzarella and arrange on top of the arugula. Tuck the sliced tomatoes around the mozzarella and scatter over the cannellini beans, basil leaves, capers, and chili strips. Dollop the lemon crème fraîche over the top, drizzle over a little olive oil, squeeze over some lemon juice, and sprinkle with a good pinch of salt and pepper to finish.

GORGONZOLA-BAKED FENNEL WITH CANNELLINI BEANS, TOMATOES, OLIVES, AND PINE NUTS

Blue cheese is one of the most polarizing foods. Some love it, many hate it. I have come full circle with my affection for blue cheese. Starting off as a hater, I now adore moldy blues for their unabashed full-flavored gutsiness. Gorgonzola, a veined Italian blue cheese, is one of my favorites—creamy, salty, and buttery, it is such a lovely accompaniment to vegetables. Here, gorgonzola is baked with fennel, in a surprising Milanese-inspired salad that just might turn you from blue cheese doubter to believer…

GF | SERVES 4~6

2 large fennel bulbs (1¾ lb; 800 g),
   trimmed and finely sliced
½ cup (125 ml) cream
½ cup (125 ml) vegetable stock
7 oz (200 g) gorgonzola, crumbled
5 thyme sprigs, leaves picked
½ lb (250 g) cherry tomatoes, halved
One and one half 15 oz cans (500 g)
   cannellini beans (about 2 cups), drained
½ cup pitted wrinkly black olives, torn
2 cups baby arugula leaves
3 tablespoons roughly chopped flat-leaf
   parsley leaves
¼ cup basil leaves, torn
3 tablespoons pine nuts, toasted
Sea salt and black pepper

SUBSTITUTE
Gorgonzola: other blue cheese variety

Preheat the oven to 400°F (200°C).

Arrange the fennel slices on a large baking tray. Stir the cream and stock together, then pour the mixture over the fennel. Scatter over the gorgonzola and thyme leaves and season with a little salt and pepper. Bake for about 20 minutes until the fennel is just tender and starting to brown. Place the cherry tomatoes on top of the fennel and bake for a further 5 minutes until the tomatoes have softened.

Combine the fennel and tomatoes with the cannellini beans, olives, arugula, and herbs. To serve, scatter over the pine nuts.

EAST,
MEET WEST

Where East meets West, salad magic is made. This is a melting pot, where influences of the West mingle with flavors from the East, creating dishes of color and flair. Geographically, Istanbul is where East meets West, a crossroads of civilizations and food. From there, we venture further afield to taste the fresh aromas of olive oil, garlic, and lemons in Lebanese cuisine and the passionate herbs and fierce spices of the Middle East. Tomatoes, cucumber, cauliflower, and eggplant synthesize gracefully with lashings of thick Greek yogurt and nutty tahini to produce powerfully flavored salads. In food, East and West exist in harmony and unity.

ROASTED CAULIFLOWER WITH FARRO, PINE NUTS, MINT, AND AGRODOLCE

I learn so much about culture and history through cooking. Agrodolce is said to have been brought to Sicily by the Arabs around the thirteenth century, a time of great cultural appreciation of Sheikh and Emirate traditions. Such experimentation at the time led to the discovery of "agro" (sour) and "dolce" (sweet) flavors that have remained strong to this day in Sicily. When I first cooked this salad for Arthur Street Kitchen, it was an instant hit. The tart sweetness of the agrodolce is quite shocking at first, but you will soon appreciate the beautiful melange of flavors, especially with hits from the mint and pine nuts.

SERVES 4~6

2 cauliflower heads (about 3½ lb; 1.5 kg), cut into florets
2–3 tablespoons extra-virgin olive oil
2½ cups (460 g) farro, rinsed
½ cup pine nuts, toasted
1 cup mint leaves, roughly torn
1 cup basil leaves, roughly torn
1½ oz (40 g) parmesan, shaved
sea salt and black pepper

AGRODOLCE DRESSING

2 teaspoons extra-virgin olive oil
1 small red onion, very finely sliced
1¼ cups (310 ml) red wine vinegar
½ cup (115 g) superfine sugar
3 tablespoons dried currants
3 black peppercorns
1 bay leaf
1 juniper berry

SUBSTITUTES/OPTIONS

Farro: pearl barley, spelt, freekeh, or quinoa
For gluten free, use quinoa in place of farro
For vegans, omit parmesan

Preheat the oven to 400°F (200°C).

Place the cauliflower florets on a large baking tray, drizzle with 1–2 tablespoons of olive oil, and season with salt. Roast for 25–30 minutes or until tender and golden.

Add the farro to a large saucepan of salted water and bring to a boil. Simmer for 30–35 minutes or until the farro grains are tender. Drain.

To make the agrodolce dressing, heat the olive oil in a saucepan, add the onion, and sauté for 3–4 minutes until it is starting to caramelize. Add the vinegar and sugar, stirring to dissolve the sugar. Finally, add the currants, peppercorns, bay leaf, and juniper berry, and simmer for 15 minutes until the sauce has reduced and is thick and syrupy. Allow to cool.

To serve, combine the cauliflower with the farro and pour over the agrodolce dressing. Season with salt and pepper and toss to combine. Drizzle over some olive oil and scatter over the pine nuts, herbs, and shaved parmesan.

SUMAC-ROASTED CAULIFLOWER WITH SPICED FREEKEH AND POMEGRANATE

I'm always looking for new flavor accents to add to roasted cauliflower and sumac is one of my favorites. The sumac bush is native to the Middle East and its deep red berries are dried and ground to produce a vibrantly hued, tangy, lemony powder. This simple cauliflower salad is full of surprises—sumac adds a lovely tart zest to the roasted cauliflower, while the pomegranate seeds deliver a surprise pop of flavor and color to every mouthful.

VG | SERVES 4~6

2 cauliflower heads (about 3½ lb; 1.5 kg), broken into small florets
4–5 tablespoons extra-virgin olive oil
2 teaspoons sumac
1 onion, finely diced
1 garlic clove, very finely chopped
1 teaspoon ground coriander
1 teaspoon ground cumin
2 cups (300 g) freekeh, rinsed
4 cups (1 liter) vegetable stock, broth or water
1 pomegranate, seeds extracted
½ cup mint leaves, torn
⅓ cup cilantro leaves
⅓ cup basil leaves, torn
1 cup walnuts, toasted
2 tablespoons pomegranate molasses
Sea salt and black pepper

SUBSTITUTES/OPTIONS
Freekeh: farro, spelt, barley, or quinoa
For gluten free, use quinoa in place of freekeh

Preheat the oven to 200°F (200°C).

Place the cauliflower florets on a large baking tray, coat in 2–3 tablespoons of olive oil, and season with salt and pepper. Sprinkle over the sumac and roast for 20–25 minutes until golden.

Heat 1 tablespoon of oil in a saucepan over medium heat, add the onion, garlic, coriander, and cumin and sauté for 1–2 minutes until softened. Add the freekeh and stock, cover with a lid, and cook for 20–25 minutes until the grains are tender. If more liquid is required, just add a bit of water.

Combine the freekeh with the cauliflower, pomegranate seeds, and herbs. Dress with a little olive oil and season with salt and pepper. To serve, scatter over the toasted walnuts and drizzle with the pomegranate molasses.

HONEY-ROASTED BRUSSELS SPROUTS WITH QUINOA AND LENTIL PILAF

Brussels sprouts and honey may not be the most obvious pairing, but once you have tasted this spunky little food combo, you will not look back! The sweetness of the honey perfectly tempers the mustardy undertones of the sprouts. Combined with this nourishing, spiced quinoa and lentil pilaf, this is a hearty salad bowl you will crave time and time again.

GF | SERVES 4~6

2¼ lb (1 kg) brussels sprouts, trimmed and halved
1–2 tablespoons extra-virgin olive oil
2 tablespoons honey
½ cup cilantro leaves
½ cup mint leaves
⅓ cup hazelnuts, roasted and roughly chopped
Sea salt and black pepper

QUINOA AND LENTIL PILAF

1 cup (200 g) green lentils, rinsed
2 tablespoons extra-virgin olive oil
1 onion, finely diced
1 garlic clove, finely chopped
2 teaspoons ground cumin
2 teaspoons ground coriander
½ teaspoon ground cinnamon
½ teaspoon ground turmeric
2 cups (300 g) red or white quinoa, rinsed
2 cups (500 ml) vegetable stock

OPTION

For vegans, use maple syrup in place of honey

Preheat the oven to 400°F (200°C).

Place the brussels sprouts on a large baking tray, drizzle over the olive oil, and season with salt and pepper. Roast for 25–30 minutes, or until tender and golden. Remove from the oven and immediately drizzle over the honey.

For the quinoa and lentil pilaf, add the lentils to a large saucepan of boiling water with a big pinch of salt. Simmer over medium heat for 20–25 minutes until soft. Drain. Heat the olive oil in a large saucepan over medium heat, add the onion and garlic, and sauté until soft. Add the spices and cook for about 30 seconds, until fragrant, then add the quinoa and stir to coat the grains in the spices. Pour over the vegetable stock, cover with a lid, and cook for 20 minutes, or until the stock has been absorbed and the quinoa is translucent. Remove from the heat and leave the pilaf to sit for 5 minutes to enable the grains to fluff up. Stir in the lentils using a fork or chopsticks.

To serve, pile the pilaf onto a large platter, top with the honey-roasted brussels sprouts, and scatter over the herbs and hazelnuts.

CHARGRILLED BRUSSELS SPROUTS AND KALE WITH CRUSHED BORLOTTI BEANS AND ZA'ATAR

This salad has so many dimensions of flavor—smoky charred brussels sprouts and crunchy roasted kale, sitting upon a bed of creamy smashed borlotti beans, topped with a healthy sprinkle of earthy za'atar. And a little tip: the crushed borlotti beans are lovely served on crostini as a starter or snack!

VG | GF | SERVES 4~6

1½ lb (700 g) brussels sprouts, trimmed
3–4 tablespoons extra-virgin olive oil
1 bunch of kale leaves, washed and dried
    thoroughly, central stems removed
    and leaves torn
½ cup pitted black olives, halved
½ cup flat-leaf parsley leaves, finely chopped
2 tablespoons za'atar
Sea salt

CRUSHED BORLOTTI BEANS

½ red onion, finely diced
3 teaspoons red wine vinegar
Three 15 oz cans (800 g) borlotti beans
    (about 3 cups), drained
2–3 tablespoons extra-virgin olive oil
Sea salt and black pepper

SUBSTITUTES

Borlotti beans: butter beans, pinto beans,
    cannellini beans

Preheat the oven to 250°F (120°C).

To prepare the crushed borlotti beans, soak the red onion in a bowl of water with 1 teaspoon of the red wine vinegar for 10 minutes (this takes the "bite" out of the onion). Drain. Add the borlotti beans to a large stainless steel bowl together with a huge pinch of salt and roughly crush using a potato masher, pestle, or large fork. Add the olive oil and crush the beans some more to a coarse, "smashed" texture (it doesn't have to be smooth). Add the remaining 2 teaspoons of red wine vinegar and the red onion and season with pepper and more salt (if required) to taste.

Depending on their size, cut each brussels sprout into 3–4 slices. Place in a large bowl, coat in 1–2 tablespoons of olive oil, and season with salt.

Heat a griddle pan, large frying pan, or barbecue to high. Add the brussels sprouts to the pan or barbecue and cook for 3 minutes on each side until tender and golden.

Place the kale leaves on a large baking tray, drizzle over 1 tablespoon of olive oil, and massage it into the leaves. Roast for 20–25 minutes until the kale leaves are crispy. Remove from the oven and sprinkle lightly with salt.

To serve, spoon the crushed borlotti beans onto a large platter, top with the sprouts and kale, and scatter over the black olives and parsley. Drizzle over a little olive oil and sprinkle over the za'atar to finish.

CUMIN-ROASTED SWEET POTATO WITH HARISSA CHICKPEAS AND SPINACH

For me, harissa is an essential kitchen condiment. I add it to everything—roasted vegetables, omelettes, pasta, sandwiches. It adds an instant lift to just about any dish. While store-bought harissa usually does the job just fine (including in this recipe), you will be surprised by the deeper flavors of the homemade variety. I like to add some dried chipotle chilies to my harissa for that extra hit of smokiness. Any extra can be topped with a thin layer of oil and stored in the fridge for up to 14 days.

VG | GF | SERVES 4~6

5 medium-large sweet potatoes
(about 4 lb; 1.75 kg), washed, unpeeled,
and cut into ½ in (1 cm) cubes
2 teaspoons cumin seeds
2–3 tablespoons extra-virgin olive oil
2 red onions, finely sliced
One and one half 15 oz cans (500 g)
chickpeas (about 2 cups), drained
3 tablespoons roughly chopped flat-leaf
parsley leaves
¼ cup cilantro leaves
2 cups baby spinach leaves
Juice of ½ lemon
3 tablespoons flaked almonds, toasted
Sea salt and black pepper

SMOKY HARISSA
(MAKES ABOUT 1 CUP/270 G)

1 large red bell pepper, halved and deseeded
⅓ cup (80 ml) extra-virgin olive oil
2–3 dried chipotle chilies, soaked in
boiling water for 30 minutes and drained
4 dry-packed sun-dried tomatoes,
rehydrated in boiling water for
30 minutes and drained
2 garlic cloves, chopped
1 teaspoon sea salt
¾ teaspoon ground coriander
½ teaspoon ground caraway
½ teaspoon ground cumin

SUBSTITUTES

Sweet potato: carrot, eggplant, squash

Preheat the oven to 400°F (200°C).

To make the harissa, begin by roasting your bell pepper. Place the pepper cut-side down on a large baking tray, drizzle with 1 tablespoon of olive oil and roast for 20–25 minutes, until the skin is charred slightly and the flesh is tender. Set aside to cool slightly, then peel away the skin. Wearing gloves, remove the seeds and stem from the soaked chipotle chilies. Place the pepper and chipotle flesh, sun-dried tomatoes, garlic, salt, spices, remaining olive oil, and 2 tablespoons of water in the bowl of a food processor and whiz together until you have a smooth, thick paste (add a little more water if it is too thick).

Place the sweet potato on a large baking tray, sprinkle over the cumin seeds, drizzle with 1–2 tablespoons of olive oil, and season with salt and pepper. Combine well and roast in the oven for 20–25 minutes until tender.

Heat 1 tablespoon of olive oil in a large frying pan, add the onions with a pinch of salt, and fry until soft, about 10 minutes. Add 4 tablespoons of harissa (or more depending on how hot you like it), the chickpeas, and a pinch of salt, and cook, stirring, for about 5 minutes until the chickpeas are well coated in the harissa and onions. Leave to cool.

Combine the sweet potato with the harissa chickpeas, herbs, and baby spinach leaves. Add a squeeze of lemon juice and table-spoons of harissa paste, season with salt and pepper, and mix well. To serve, scatter over the almonds.

ISRAELI CHOPPED SALAD WITH TOMATOES, CUCUMBER, RADISH, AND FETA

Over the years, I have had the good fortune to have many friends guide me in the art of an Israeli salad. The first was my good friend Gabi, who, in my old hood of Surry Hills, would nonchalantly whip up this fresh, colorful chopped tomato and cucumber salad with a dollop of cottage cheese. In Brooklyn, my new pals Leetal and Ron at NY Shuk furthered my love of this insanely simple salad, daring me to push the boundaries with lemon and olive oil. Everyone has their own version of Israeli salad, but, learning from the best, this is my simple version.

GF | SERVES 4~6

3 large beefsteak tomatoes (about 2 lb; 1 kg),
   or other seasonal variety
4 small Lebanese cucumbers
   (about 1 lb; 400 g), trimmed
1 bunch of radishes (about ¾ lb; 300 g),
   trimmed
1 red onion
3–4 green onion (see note page 32)
1 cup flat-leaf parsley leaves
½ cup mint leaves
½ cup cilantro leaves
1 long green chili, deseeded and
   finely chopped
Juice of 1–2 lemons
About ¾ cup (200 ml) extra-virgin olive oil
7 oz (200 g) sheep's milk feta, crumbled
Sea salt and black pepper

If the tomatoes and cucumber have lots of seeds, cut them out and discard. Cut the tomatoes into roughly ¼ in (5 mm) cubes, followed by the cucumbers, radishes, and red onion, making sure everything is about the same size. Chop the green onions, parsley, mint, and cilantro leaves as finely as possible. Place everything in a large mixing bowl and add in the chili.

Now it is time to dress the salad with the lemon juice and olive oil. I encourage you to add these gradually—tasting, adding more, and tasting again—until you achieve the acidity you like. Remember, this salad is designed to be very lemony.

To serve, season well with salt and pepper. Taste and add more lemon juice, if you like, and scatter over the crumbled feta.

CHARGRILLED EGGPLANT AND LENTILS WITH ARUGULA, HERB TAHINI, AND POMEGRANATE

Herb tahini is such a versatile addition to any home cook's repertoire. Add whichever herbs you have on hand. I have used parsley and mint for a lovely earthy addition, but you could also use cilantro, oregano, basil, chives, or a combination of all. This herb tahini is also a great dip for crackers or vegetable crudité. Eggplant and lentils is one of my all-time favorite vegetable-legume combos.

GF | SERVES 4~6

5 eggplants (4½ lb; 2 kg), sliced into
   ½ in (1 cm) thick rounds
2–3 tablespoons extra-virgin olive oil
1½ cups (300 g) brown lentils, rinsed
1 cup baby arugula leaves
½ cup mint leaves
½ cup cilantro leaves
½ cup flat-leaf parsley leaves,
   roughly chopped
1 pomegranate, seeds extracted
Sea salt and black pepper

HERB TAHINI

½ cup flat-leaf parsley leaves,
   roughly chopped
½ cup mint leaves, roughly torn
1 long green chili, deseeded
1 small garlic clove, very finely chopped
1 cup (135 g) tahini paste
Juice of ½ lemon
1 tablespoon honey
3 tablespoons extra-virgin olive oil
Sea salt and black pepper

OPTION

For vegans, use maple syrup in place
   of honey

To make the herb tahini, place the herbs, chili, garlic, and tahini paste in the bowl of a food processor and whiz together until almost smooth. Add the lemon juice and honey and pulse together again. With the motor on, slowly drizzle in the olive oil and about 1–2 tablespoons of water until the tahini is the consistency of heavy whipping cream. Season with salt and pepper.

Heat a griddle pan or barbecue to high. In a large bowl, coat the eggplant slices in the olive oil. Add the eggplant to the pan or barbecue and cook for about 2–3 minutes on each side until tender and charred. Remove and leave to cool slightly. When cool enough to handle, slice into finger-sized pieces and season well with salt and pepper.

Tip the lentils into a saucepan of water and bring to a boil. Add a big pinch of salt to the water and cook for 20–25 minutes, until the lentils are just tender. Drain.

Combine the eggplant with the lentils, arugula, and herbs and fold through the herb tahini. Serve topped with pomegranate seeds.

EGGPLANT WITH HALOUMI, BEET TZATZIKI, AND YOGURT FLATBREADS

One of my lasting memories of traveling in Turkey was the ubiquitous vegetable dishes smothered in yogurt. This salad takes inspiration from the grandeur of creamy yogurt-covered eggplant in Turkish cuisine, with a naturally vibrant beet-tinged tzatziki adding a color-popping surprise. Serve with salty, chewy haloumi and these life-changing flatbreads and you'll have a new family favorite! This flatbread is simple to make and terrific cooked on a barbecue. As a time-saver, use pre-cooked whole beets.

SERVES 4~6

4 eggplants (about 3½; 1.6 kg)
4–5 tablespoons extra-virgin olive oil
12 oz (350 g) haloumi, cut into ¼ in (5 mm)
   thick slices
2 cups baby spinach leaves
1 cup walnuts, toasted and crushed
½ cup mint leaves, torn
½ cup cilantro leaves
Sea salt and black pepper
Lemon wedges, to serve

YOGURT FLATBREADS

1 cup (240 g) natural yogurt
1 teaspoon sea salt
2¼ cups (330 g) self-rising flour,
   plus extra for dusting

BEET TZATZIKI

2 small beets (about ½ lb; 250 g), peeled
1 teaspoon cumin seeds
1 small garlic clove, chopped
1½ cups (375 g) Greek yogurt
1 teaspoon honey
1 tablespoon chopped dill
2 tablespoons chopped mint leaves
Juice of ½ lemon
2 teaspoons extra-virgin olive oil
Sea salt and black pepper

SUBSTITUTES

Eggplant: cauliflower
Haloumi: feta (unfried)

Preheat the oven to 400°F (200°C).

For the flatbread, combine the yogurt and salt in a large bowl and beat until smooth. Gradually add the flour, stirring, until a stiff dough forms. On a lightly floured surface, knead the dough, adding a little more flour if needed, until soft and slightly sticky. Place the dough in a lightly oiled bowl, cover with plastic wrap, and leave to rest for 30 minutes.

For the beet tzatziki, place the beets in a small saucepan and cover with water. Bring to a boil, cover, and simmer for 20–25 minutes or until the beets are tender. Drain and leave to cool, then finely grate. Toast the cumin seeds in a dry frying pan until fragrant, then add to a bowl along with the beets and remaining tzatziki ingredients. Season with salt and pepper, mix together well, and transfer to the refrigerator to chill.

Peel strips of skin from the eggplants, from top to bottom, so it leaves a stripy pattern. Cut the eggplants into 1 in (2 cm) cubes and arrange on a large baking tray in a single layer. Drizzle with 2–3 tablespoons of olive oil and roast for 25–30 minutes until soft and golden. Remove from the oven and season with salt.

Place the flatbread dough on a floured surface and divide it into six balls. Roll each ball into a 6 in (16 cm) circle. Brush each side with olive oil and sprinkle with a little salt. Heat a frying pan over a medium-high heat, add the flatbreads to the pan one at a time and cook for 30–40 seconds on each side until they puff up and are golden in parts. Turn and repeat on the other side—don't overcook.

When almost ready to serve, brush each side of the haloumi with olive oil and cook on a griddle pan, large frying pan, or barbecue. Cook for 1–2 minutes on each side until soft and golden.

To serve, spread the beet tzatziki generously over a serving platter. Combine the eggplant with the spinach, walnuts, and herbs, and spoon it over the tzatziki. Drizzle with olive oil and season with a pinch of salt and pepper. Serve with the haloumi, flatbread, and some lemon wedges on the side, or roll everything up in the flatbread.

LEBANESE STEWED GREEN BEANS AND CHICKPEAS WITH SPINACH PILAF

If ever a salad embodied comfort, it would surely be this one. The simplest of ingredients—green beans, tomatoes, and chickpeas—combine to create the most spectacular of flavors. This salad, inspired by Lebanese-style stewed beans, is even better the next day, so plan ahead if you can. The spinach and bulgur wheat pilaf is good enough to scoff all on its own!

VG | SERVES 4~6

1–2 tablespoons extra-virgin olive oil
1 tablespoon cumin seeds
1 teaspoon coriander seeds
1 onion, finely diced
2 garlic cloves, very finely chopped
3 tablespoons tomato paste
1½ lb (700 g) green beans, trimmed
One half 15 oz can (250 g) cooked chickpeas
    (about ½ cup), drained
One 15 oz can (400 g) diced tomatoes
    (about 1 cup)
½ cup cilantro leaves, roughly chopped
3 tablespoons slivered almonds, toasted
Sea salt and black pepper

SPINACH PILAF

1–2 tablespoons extra-virgin olive oil
1 small red onion, finely diced
1 garlic clove, very finely chopped
2¾ cups (400 g) bulgur wheat
    (cracked wheat)
3 cups (750 ml) vegetable stock or broth
3 cups baby spinach leaves, washed
    thoroughly and roughly chopped
Sea salt

Heat the olive oil in a large casserole dish, add the cumin and coriander seeds, and cook, stirring often, for about 1 minute or until the seeds are popping and fragrant. Add the onion and garlic, season well with salt and pepper, and sauté until the onion is soft and golden, about 3–4 minutes. Add the tomato paste and cook for a further 2 minutes, then add the green beans, chickpeas, tomatoes, and ⅓ cup (80 ml) of water. Bring to a boil, then reduce to a simmer, cover, and cook for 45–60 minutes over medium heat until the beans are very tender. Remove from the heat, season with salt and pepper to taste, and leave to cool.

While the green beans are cooling, make the pilaf. In a large saucepan, heat the olive oil over medium heat, add the onion and garlic, and cook until the onion is soft and translucent, about 3–4 minutes. Add the bulgur wheat and stir to coat the grains in the hot oil. Pour over the vegetable stock and add a pinch of salt, then reduce the heat to low, cover with a lid, and leave to cook for about 10 minutes. The pilaf is ready when all the liquid has been absorbed. When cooked, remove the lid and fold through the spinach leaves, then place a clean tea towel over the pan and replace the lid. Leave to stand and steam for 15 minutes (the residual heat will wilt the spinach).

To serve, combine the stewed beans and chickpeas with the pilaf. Sprinkle over the cilantro and almonds to finish.

CHERMOULA-ROASTED ORANGE VEGETABLES
WITH CHICKPEAS AND COUSCOUS

Orange is the new black? In this salad, orange is definitely the hottest color around. Butternut squash, carrots, sweet potatoes, and orange bell peppers (though yellow are fine if you can't find orange!) are rubbed and roasted in chermoula, a heady spice rub commonly used in Tunisian, Moroccan, Libyan, and Algerian cooking. Chermoula is classically served with couscous and chickpeas, as it is here in this salad. Make the chermoula in advance and store in the refrigerator for up to 5 days.

SERVES 4~6

1 cup (185 g) couscous
2 tablespoons extra-virgin olive oil
1½ cups (375 ml) boiling vegetable stock
   or broth
1 small butternut squash (about 1¾ lb; 800 g),
   peeled and cut into 1 in (2 cm) chunks
2 sweet potatoes (about 1 lb; 500 g), cut into
   1 in (2 cm) chunks
3 carrots (about ¾ lb; 350 g), peeled and
   cut into 1 in (2 cm) chunks
3 orange bell peppers, deseeded and
   cut into 1 in (2 cm) chunks
2 tomatoes, roughly chopped
2 tablespoons honey
Juice of ½ lemon
One and one half 15 oz cans (500 g) cooked
   chickpeas (about 2 cups), drained
½ cup flat-leaf parsley leaves, finely chopped
½ cup cilantro leaves, finely chopped
3 tablespoons slivered almonds, toasted
Sea salt and black pepper

CHERMOULA

2 garlic cloves
2 teaspoons ground cumin
2 teaspoons paprika
½ teaspoon cayenne pepper
Zest and juice of 1 lemon
1 teaspoon sea salt
3 tablespoons extra-virgin olive oil
½ cup flat-leaf parsley leaves, finely chopped
½ cup cilantro leaves, finely chopped

OPTIONS

For gluten free, use quinoa or millet
   in place of couscous
For vegans, omit honey

To make the chermoula, using a mortar and pestle, pound together the garlic, cumin, paprika, cayenne, lemon zest, lemon juice, and salt. Whisk in the olive oil until well combined. Stir in the parsley and cilantro. Alternatively, you can use a food processor to mix together all the ingredients.

Preheat the oven to 250°F (120°C).

Put the couscous into a shallow bowl along with 1 tablespoon of olive oil and stir through to coat the grains. Pour over the vegetable stock and stir well. Cover the bowl with plastic wrap and let stand for 10 minutes. Uncover, drizzle with the remaining olive oil, and stir together, then cover with foil and heat in the oven for 5 minutes. Remove from the oven and fluff up the grains with a fork.

Increase the oven temperature to 400°F (200°C).

Place the squash, sweet potato, carrots, bell peppers and tomatoes on a large baking tray. Add enough of the chermoula to generously coat the vegetables (keeping the remainder aside for later) and rub it into the vegetables with your hands. Season with a pinch of salt and pepper and roast for 30–35 minutes until the vegetables are tender. Remove from the oven, immediately drizzle over the honey, and squeeze over the lemon juice.

To serve, add the remaining chermoula to the vegetables and stir through. Combine the vegetables with the couscous, chickpeas, and herbs. Season with salt and pepper and top with the almonds.

MOGHRABIEH WITH BLACK LENTILS AND SUGAR SNAP PEAS

Hailing from the Middle East, moghrabieh grains are like oversized couscous, made of semolina and formed into small, pasta-like balls. In Lebanon, moghrabieh, which is traditionally served with meat, is a feasting dish, a meal to share with family and friends. Here, I have taken the feasting to a new level, teaming hearty moghrabieh grains with fortifying black lentils, crispy-sweet, raw sugar snap peas, and the most refreshing seasonal herbs.

VG | SERVES 4~6

2 cups (400 g) moghrabieh
1 garlic clove, very finely chopped
5 cups (1.25 liters) vegetable stock
½ cup (100 g) black lentils, rinsed
1 lb (400 g) sugar snap peas, trimmed and
　cut into very thin strips
½ cup flat-leaf parsley leaves,
　roughly chopped
½ cup mint leaves, roughly chopped
½ cup cilantro leaves, roughly chopped
½ cup finely chopped green onion (see
　note page 32)
Juice of 1–2 lemons
3–4 tablespoons extra-virgin olive oil
Sea salt and black pepper

SUBSTITUTES

Moghrabieh: pearl couscous, fregola
Black lentils: brown, green or puy lentils
Sugar snap peas: snow peas

Add the moghrabieh balls, chopped garlic, and vegetable stock to a saucepan. Bring to a boil, then lower the heat to a rolling simmer and leave to cook for 20–25 minutes until the moghrabieh balls are al dente. Take off the heat, drain off the remaining liquid, and run under cold water. Set aside to dry out a little.

In a medium saucepan, add the lentils and cover with plenty of cold water. Add a big pinch of sea salt. Bring to a boil, reduce the heat, and cook for 20–25 minutes until just tender. Drain.

Using a very sharp knife, finely slice the sugar snap peas into razor-thin strips.

Combine the moghrabieh, lentils, pea strips, and herbs. Dress with the lemon juice and olive oil and season well with salt and pepper. Taste and adjust the quantities of lemon juice and oil to achieve a balanced, tangy dressing.

BEET, KOHLRABI, CARROT, AND
APPLE SLAW WITH LABNEH

Labneh sounds exotic, but it is actually just strained yogurt. As simple as it is to create, homemade labneh never fails to impress. You can get fancy and roll it into balls, cover in dukkah or za'atar, and marinate in oil. You can add finely chopped radishes, carrots, and shallots to create a flavorsome vegetable dip. Or you can just dollop it on top of salads, like I have here. In this salad, the creamy, slightly tart hum of the labneh completely enlivens this sweet and colorful raw party of beet, kohlrabi, carrot, and apple.

GF | SERVES 4~6

1 kohlrabi (about ¾ cup; 350 g), peeled
2 beets (about ¾ cup; 350 g), peeled
2 carrots (about ¾ cup; 350 g), peeled
2 apples (about 1 lb; 500 g), peeled
½ cup mint leaves
½ cup cilantro leaves
½ cup flat-leaf parsley leaves
3 tablespoons squash seeds, toasted

LABNEH

2 cups (500 g) Greek yogurt
1 garlic clove, grated
Sea salt and black pepper

SHERRY VINEGAR DRESSING

Juice of ½ lemon
2 tablespoons extra-virgin olive oil
2 tablespoons sherry vinegar
2 teaspoons superfine sugar
Sea salt

SUBSTITUTE

Kohlrabi: zucchini

Labneh needs making a day before you want to serve it and keeps in the fridge for 5 days, or longer if marinated. To make it, line a colander or sieve with a piece of muslin or a thin cotton sheet. Combine the yogurt and garlic together with a pinch of salt and pepper, spoon it into the cloth, and secure tightly with an elastic band or tie. Give the bundle a good squeeze over the sink, then put it back into the colander. Sit the colander over a shallow plate or bowl and leave it in the fridge for at least 24 hours. During this time, the yogurt will lose its excess moisture, leaving a firmer mixture a bit like cream cheese. If you can, squeeze out any excess liquid from time to time to help this firming process.

To make the dressing, combine the lemon juice, olive oil, sherry vinegar, sugar, and a pinch of sea salt in a small saucepan. Bring to a simmer and stir until the sugar and salt have fully dissolved. Set aside.

Using a mandoline, food processor, or box grater, shave or grate the vegetables and apple into thin strips (leaving the apple for last as it will brown).

Place the shredded fruit and vegetables in a large bowl and immediately drizzle over the warm dressing. Add the herbs, season with salt and pepper, and gently toss the salad with your hands. To serve, dot with big balls or spoonfuls of labneh and sprinkle over the squash seeds.

LENTILS, LEEKS, RICE, AND CARAMELIZED ONIONS
WITH LEMON-TOMATO OKRA

When I was about fifteen, I started to experiment in the kitchen with foods from other cultures. One of the first meals I cooked for myself was a mujaddara recipe from my Australian Women's Weekly *Middle Eastern cookbook. I remember being entranced by the flavors of this very simple Lebanese dish of rice, lentils, and caramelized onions. This is my version, with leeks and a lemon-laced okra. The lemon in the okra serves a double purpose—it adds a lovely zestiness and also, as I learned from my good friend Sneh Roy from the blog* Cook Republic, *it also eliminates some of okra's sliminess!*

VG | GF | SERVES 4~6

3 tablespoons extra-virgin olive oil

3 leeks, white and light green parts only, finely sliced and washed

1 garlic clove, finely chopped

2 cups (400 g) basmati rice, rinsed

2 teaspoons ground cumin

1 teaspoon ground allspice

½ teaspoon cayenne pepper

1 cup (200 g) brown lentils, rinsed

2 bay leaves

2 cinnamon sticks

6 cups (1.5 liters) vegetable stock

6 brown onions, halved and finely sliced

1 teaspoon superfine sugar

1 cup cilantro leaves

Sea salt and black pepper

LEMON-TOMATO OKRA

1 tablespoon extra-virgin olive oil

2 garlic cloves, finely chopped

1 teaspoon ground cumin

1 lb (400 g) okra, washed and trimmed

4 roma tomatoes (about 1 lb; 500 g), cut into ½ in (1 cm) dice

Juice of 1 lemon

Sea salt

Heat 2 tablespoons of olive oil in a casserole dish or large saucepan over medium heat. Add the leeks, season with a pinch of salt, and sauté for 7–8 minutes until soft and golden. Add the garlic and rice and cook for 2 minutes, then stir in the cumin, allspice, and cayenne pepper and cook for 30 seconds. Add the lentils, bay leaves, and cinnamon sticks and stir in the vegetable stock. Bring to a steady simmer, cover, and cook for 20 minutes or so, until the rice and lentils are both cooked and the liquid has been absorbed. Remove the lid, discard the bay leaves, and cinnamon stick and leave to cool.

Meanwhile, heat 1 tablespoon of olive oil in a frying pan and add the onions, sugar and a big pinch of salt. Sauté over medium heat for 15–20 minutes, until the onions are golden and caramelized.

For the lemon-tomato okra, heat the olive oil in a large frying pan over a high heat, add the garlic and cumin, and fry for 10 seconds until fragrant. Add the okra with a pinch of salt and fry for 5 minutes, until tender and golden. Stir in the tomatoes along with 2 tablespoons of water and cook for another 5 minutes until the tomatoes are just soft. Take off the heat and squeeze in the lemon juice.

To serve, transfer the rice and lentil mixture onto a large serving platter, spoon over the lemon okra, and top with the caramelized onions. Scatter over the cilantro leaves.

TO ASIA, WITH LOVE

Asian fare is my comfort food. Though I was born and raised in Sydney, I am Chinese deep in my heart. The flavors of my childhood still transport me to my happy place. When I am homesick or need a big hit of flavor, I always turn to dumplings, a rambling bowl of noodles, braised shiitake mushrooms with tofu, or stir-fried broccoli. Now, Asian salads are my favorite dishes to make, affording me the ultimate opportunity to flex my multicultural muscle—I can experiment with a deep umami dressing, splash out with something spicy or adorned with peanuts, pursue a dish with a tropical twist, or opt for a finish that is a little sweet and a little savory. In an Asian salad, there is heart, home, and love.

BRUSSELS SPROUTS WITH STIR-FRIED LOTUS ROOT, BLACK FUNGUS, FIVE-SPICE TOFU, AND HOISIN-SESAME SAUCE

Even if I'm on the other side of the world, the bustle of the local Chinatown is where I feel closest to my family. When I'm in a foreign city, I habitually seek out rustic-looking Chinese restaurants to listen to the locals speak Cantonese and to take in the distinctive Chinatown aromas that are somehow the same, no matter where I am! This salad is inspired by the unabashed flavors of Cantonese cuisine.

VG | SERVES 4~6

1½ lb (700 g) brussels sprouts, trimmed and halved

2–3 tablespoons extra-virgin olive oil

2½ oz (75 g) black wood ear fungus

14 oz (400 g) frozen lotus root, defrosted for 30 minutes

7 oz (220 g) five-spice tofu, finely sliced into thin strips

3 tablespoons finely sliced green onion (see note page 32)

3 tablespoons roughly chopped cilantro leaves

1 tablespoon white sesame seeds, toasted

1 tablespoon black sesame seeds

3 tablespoons crispy fried shallots

Sea salt and black pepper

HOISIN-SESAME SAUCE

3 tablespoons hoisin sauce

3 tablespoons tahini paste

1 tablespoon sesame oil

1 tablespoon rice bran oil (or other neutral oil)

1 garlic clove, grated

Sea salt and black pepper

SUBSTITUTES

Frozen lotus root: fresh lotus root, water chestnuts, bamboo shoots

Black fungus: shiitake mushrooms

Five-spice tofu: pan-fried firm tofu

Preheat the oven to 400°F (200°C).

Place the halved brussels sprouts on a large baking tray, drizzle with 1–2 tablespoons of olive oil, and season well with salt and pepper. Roast the brussels sprouts for 25–30 minutes until slightly charred and tender.

To make the sauce, combine the hoisin sauce and tahini paste, then slowly add 3 tablespoons of water, stirring as you go. Add the sesame oil, rice bran oil, and garlic, and stir together until well combined. Season well with salt and pepper.

Soak the black fungus in hot water for 15 minutes. Drain and dry with a tea towel and tear the larger pieces in half. Carefully pick through the fungus to remove any hard stems or debris. Heat 1 tablespoon of olive oil in a large frying pan or wok, add the lotus root (careful, the oil will spit!), and fry for 3–4 minutes until mostly defrosted. Add the black fungus and a big pinch of salt and stir-fry until the lotus root is cooked through and has taken on some color, about 5 minutes. You will hear the fungus crackle and pop in the pan, which is normal.

Combine the brussels sprouts with the lotus root, black fungus, tofu, and herbs. Add the sauce and toss well. Scatter over the sesame seeds and top with the crispy fried shallots.

THAI CARROT AND PEANUT SALAD

For me, home is where I am close to a great local Thai eatery. Having left Sydney, home to so many wonderful, inexpensive Thai restaurants, one of my first missions in my new neighborhood of Carroll Gardens in Brooklyn was to find my local Thai joint. And just a few blocks away, I found it. One day, over lunch with my kids, I tasted a smashing peanut sauce that inspired me to create this salad. This dish features raw shredded carrot, crisp bean sprouts, and tofu, escorted by a punchy peanut sauce.

GF | SERVES 4~6

32 oz (800 g) firm tofu, cut into ½ in (1 cm)
    thick slices
1 tablespoon olive oil
10 small carrots (about 2 lbs; 1 kg), peeled
½ lb (180 g) bean sprouts
1 kaffir lime leaf, very finely sliced
3 cups Asian herb leaves (Thai basil,
    cilantro, green onion, Vietnamese mint,
    or perilla)
½ cup roasted peanuts, roughly chopped
Sea salt and black pepper

SPICY PEANUT SAUCE

½ cup (120 g) peanut butter
1½ in (3 cm) piece of ginger, peeled
    and grated
3 tablespoons honey
½ teaspoon superfine sugar
1 tablespoon tamari
2 tablespoons vegetable oil
1 tablespoon sesame oil
2 tablespoons rice wine vinegar
Juice of 1 lime
Small pinch of chili flakes
Sea salt

To make the spicy peanut sauce, combine all the ingredients in the bowl of a food processor and whiz together to form a creamy sauce. Alternatively, combine the ingredients together in a small bowl with a whisk. Add a splash of water if it is too thick—you want the consistency of pouring cream. Season with salt to taste.

Coat the tofu slices in the olive oil and season well with salt and pepper. Heat a large frying pan over medium heat, add the tofu slices, and fry for 3–4 minutes on each side until golden. Leave to cool completely, then slice the tofu into thin strips.

Using a mandoline, grater attachment on your food processor, or box grater, grate the carrots into thin strips.

Combine the carrots with the bean sprouts, tofu strips, kaffir lime leaf, and herbs and toss well. Add the peanut sauce and toss again. To serve, top with the peanuts.

ROASTED BEETS WITH QUINOA, SHALLOTS, AND ORANGE MISO

Miso is such a wonderful pantry staple. And it is surprisingly versatile in salad-making. In this salad, the umami goodness of the slightly sweet, slightly citrus orange miso really brings out the earthy worldliness of the beets. Use whatever beets are in season, whether they be regular crimsons, goldens, target beets, or baby varieties. If your beets have lovely green tops, reserve them for your salad.

VG | GF | SERVES 4~6

8 small beets (about 2 lbs; 1 kg), peeled and
    cut into 1 in (2 cm) cubes, leaves reserved
    and torn
4 shallots (see note page 32), peeled and
    finely sliced
2 tablespoons extra-virgin olive oil
2¼ cups (400 g) white or red quinoa, rinsed
3 cups (750 ml) vegetable stock, broth
    or water
3 tablespoons roughly chopped flat-leaf
    parsley leaves
½ cup cilantro leaves
½ cup slivered almonds, toasted (optional)
Sea salt and black pepper

ORANGE-MISO DRESSING

3 tablespoons miso paste
1 tablespoon sesame oil
1 garlic clove, grated
About 1 in (2.5 cm) piece of ginger, peeled
    and grated
1 tablespoon maple syrup
½ cup (125 ml) freshly squeezed
    orange juice

SUBSTITUTE

Beet leaves: baby arugula leaves

Preheat the oven to 400°F (200°C).

Combine the beets with the shallots and spread over a large baking tray. Drizzle over the olive oil and season with salt and pepper. Roast for 25–30 minutes until the beets are tender.

Placed the rinsed quinoa in a large saucepan and add the vegetable stock and a big pinch of salt. Bring to a boil, then lower the heat and simmer for 15–20 minutes until the quinoa is tender and translucent. When cooked, turn off the heat and leave the quinoa to sit uncovered in the pan for 10 minutes, to allow the grains to separate and dry out.

To make the dressing, whisk together all the ingredients until well combined.

Combine the beets, beet leaves, shallots, quinoa, and herbs with the dressing and toss well. To serve, top with the almonds, if using.

ROASTED CARROTS WITH GREEN BEANS, MUNG BEANS, AND COCONUT DUKKAH

It is so satisfying to make a batch of dukkah. So expensive to buy, but so simple to make at home, I always have some on hand to top roasted vegetables, salads, or even sandwiches. This coconut dukkah was the result of a little kitchen experiment when I was craving coconut. It adds a tropical, South-East Asian feel to the salad. This recipe makes a generous amount of coconut dukkah, more than you will need for this recipe—keep extra in the pantry or give it as a gift (if you don't want extra, simply halve the recipe).

VG | GF | SERVES 4~6

1 red onion, finely sliced
4–5 tablespoons extra-virgin olive oil
10 carrots (about 3½ lb; 1.5 kg), sliced
    diagonally
1½ cups (300 g) dried mung beans
½ cup (250 g) green beans, trimmed
½ cup cilantro leaves
¼ cup flat-leaf parsley leaves
3 tablespoons finely sliced green onion
    (see note page 32)
Juice of ½ lemon
Sea salt and black pepper

COCONUT DUKKAH (MAKES 1 CUP)

4 white peppercorns
2 tablespoons coriander seeds
2 tablespoons cumin seeds
½ cup almonds or shelled pistachios, toasted
½ cup (45 g) desiccated coconut, toasted
2 tablespoons white sesame seeds, toasted
1 tablespoon black sesame seeds
1 tablespoon nigella seeds
1 teaspoon sea salt

SUBSTITUTE

Desiccated coconut: fresh coconut

Preheat the oven to 400°F (200°C).

To make the coconut dukkah, place a frying pan over medium heat and toast the peppercorns and the coriander and cumin seeds until fragrant and popping, about 60 seconds. Add to a mortar and pound with a pestle to a coarse powder, then add the nuts and pound again until chunky. Mix through the coconut, sesame seeds, nigella seeds, and salt.

Coat the red onion slices in 2 teaspoons of olive oil and set aside. Place the carrots on a large baking tray, coat in 1–2 tablespoons of olive oil, season with salt and pepper, and place in the oven to roast. After 20 minutes, add the sliced red onion to the baking tray and roast for a further 10 minutes or until the carrots and onion are both tender and golden.

Bring a saucepan of salted water to a boil, add the mung beans and simmer for 25–30 minutes until tender. Drain.

In a large frying pan, add 1 tablespoon of olive oil and fry the green beans until just tender and starting to color. Remove from the pan.

Combine the carrots, mung beans, green beans, herbs, a drizzle of olive oil, and a good squeeze of lemon juice, and season with salt and pepper to taste. Scatter over the coconut dukkah and serve.

EDAMAME BEANS WITH BABY BOK CHOY, QUINOA, AND HONEY-GINGER DRESSING

This salad is inspired by an afternoon of cooking with photographer and author Karen Mordechai at the incomparable Sunday Suppers in Williamsburg, Brooklyn. Karen kindly invited me to her stunning community kitchen to cook a salad. I brought along some local Greenmarket finds and she raided her pantry. That day, we cooked an Asian-inspired salad, similar to this dish. Feel free to use your favorite Asian greens and, if you can find them, definitely use fresh soy beans.

GF | SERVES 4~6

1 teaspoon vegetable stock powder
2¼ cups (400 g) white or red quinoa, rinsed
1 teaspoon sesame oil
1 tablespoon extra-virgin olive oil
1 lb (400 g) frozen podded edamame beans
4–5 bunches of baby bok choy,
　leaves separated
2 tablespoons white sesame seeds, toasted
2 tablespoons black sesame seeds
½ cup cilantro leaves
Sea salt and white pepper

HONEY-GINGER DRESSING

1 in (2.5 cm) piece of ginger, peeled
1 small garlic clove
1 tablespoon honey
1 tablespoon rice wine vinegar
2 tablespoons mirin
1 tablespoon sesame oil
3 tablespoons extra-virgin olive oil
Sea salt and white pepper

SUBSTITUTES

Baby bok choy: choy sum, Chinese broccoli,
　tatsoi

To make the dressing, using a Microplane or the finest setting on a box grater, finely grate the ginger and garlic. Place in a bowl with the honey, vinegar, mirin, and oils and whisk together. Add a pinch of salt, taste, and adjust the seasoning if required.

Add the stock powder, quinoa, a pinch of salt, and 3 cups (750 ml) of water to a saucepan. Bring to a boil, then reduce to a simmer and cook for 15–20 minutes, or until all the liquid has been absorbed and the quinoa is translucent. Turn the heat off and leave the quinoa to sit, uncovered, for 10 minutes to allow the grains to separate and dry out.

Heat the oils in a large frying pan or wok. Add the edamame beans with a pinch of salt and a splash of water and stir-fry for 3–4 minutes, then throw in the bok choy leaves and stir-fry for a further minute, until the leaves are just wilted but still bright green and the edamame are tender.

Combine the edamame beans and bok choy with the quinoa and season with salt and white pepper. Add the honey-ginger dressing and toss well. To serve, scatter over the sesame seeds and cilantro leaves.

PHO NOODLE SALAD WITH TOFU, NAPA CABBAGE, AND BROCCOLINI

When we lived in Sydney, my family would often head over to the neighborhood of Marrickville to have a bowl of pho. Well, for the others, not me! I would covetously sit by and literally salivate over the intoxicating bouquet of cinnamon, cloves, ginger, and star anise! Having been a vegetarian for over twenty years, pho noodle soup is really one of the only meat dishes that tempts me. So here, I bring my flesh-free pho dreams to life in an irresistible noodle salad.

VG | GF | SERVES 4~6

¾ lb (350 g) thick dried rice noodles
1 tablespoon extra-virgin olive oil
1 lb (400 g) broccolini, trimmed and sliced
   diagonally into 1 in (2.5 cm) pieces
¼ lb (120 g) Napa cabbage, finely sliced
7 oz (220 g) five-spice tofu, finely sliced into
   thin strips
½ lb (180 g) bean sprouts
1 cup Asian herb leaves (Thai basil, cilantro,
   green onion, Vietnamese mint, or perilla)
1 long red chili, finely chopped (optional)
1 lime, cut into wedges
Sea salt and white pepper

PHO DRESSING

2 onions, peeled and halved
3 in (7 cm) piece of ginger, peeled and
   halved lengthways
1 cinnamon stick
5 white peppercorns
3 star anise
3 whole cloves
1 teaspoon coriander seeds
6 cups (1.5 liters) vegetable stock or water
1 tablespoon tamari
6 carrots, peeled and coarsely chopped
3 dried shiitake mushrooms
3 tablespoons extra-virgin olive oil
Sea salt

SUBSTITUTES

Broccolini: broccoli
Napa cabbage: green cabbage

To make the dressing, place the onions and ginger pieces directly on the flame of a gas stovetop or under a very hot grill until they are slightly blackened all over. Heat a large saucepan over a medium-low heat. Add the cinnamon, peppercorns, star anise, cloves, and coriander seeds and toast, stirring to prevent burning, for 30 seconds until aromatic. Add the vegetable stock, tamari, carrots, mushrooms, charred onion, and ginger to the pan and bring to a boil, then reduce the heat to low and simmer, uncovered, for 60–80 minutes until reduced by a third. Strain. Season with salt to taste and whisk in the olive oil.

Bring a large saucepan of salted water to a boil, add the rice noodles and cook for 6–8 minutes until tender. Drain and refresh under cold running water.

In a frying pan, add the olive oil and pan-fry the broccolini for about 5 minutes, until just tender and lightly charred.

Combine the noodles, cabbage, broccolini, tofu, bean sprouts, and herbs and pour over some of the dressing. Mix together well, making sure everything is coated in the dressing and season with salt and white pepper. Serve topped with chopped chili (if you like) and lime wedges.

SEEDY SOBA NOODLES WITH ASIAN HERBS

Soba, with its robust texture and hearty buckwheat flavor, is the consummate salad noodle. While I religiously enjoy most of my salads at room temperature, I like my soba chilled. This salad was created for the love of texture: smooth, silky cold noodles loaded up with whatever seeds you can think of and a host of Asian herbs that really take center stage.

SERVES 4~6

1 lb (500 g) soba noodles
1–2 tablespoons olive oil
1 cup cilantro leaves
½ cup Thai basil or regular basil leaves
½ cup Vietnamese mint or regular
   mint leaves
½ cup finely chopped green onion
   (see note page 32)
1 cup sunflower seeds, toasted
1 cup squash seeds, toasted
½ cup white sesame seeds, toasted
½ cup black sesame seeds
3 tablespoons nigella seeds
Sea salt and white pepper

SWEET GINGER DRESSING

1 in (3 cm) piece of ginger, peeled and grated
1 garlic clove, grated
2 tablespoons honey
3 tablespoons extra-virgin olive oil
2 tablespoons sesame oil
1 tablespoon cider vinegar
Sea salt and white pepper

SUBSTITUTES

Soba noodles: mung bean vermicelli,
   rice noodles

Bring a large pot of salted water to a boil, add the soba noodles, and cook for 3–4 minutes, stirring constantly to prevent sticking, until just tender. Drain and refresh under cold running water. Place the noodles in the fridge for at least 1 hour to chill.

To make the dressing, mix together the ginger and garlic in a small bowl. Add the remaining ingredients and whisk everything together. Season with salt and white pepper.

To serve, place the chilled noodles in a large bowl and loosen them up with the olive oil (any variety is okay). Roughly chop or tear the herb leaves and add them to the bowl with the green onion, seeds, and dressing. Toss gently to combine and season with salt and white pepper.

LEMONGRASS TOFU WITH ASIAN GREENS AND MUNG BEAN VERMICELLI

I have a strong affection for lemongrass and not only because of its tropical, citrus scent and its potent medicinal qualities. Lemongrass also reminds me of the suburban Sydney house where I grew up. We always had lemongrass growing in our backyard and later, when we lived in Surry Hills, my mother supplied lemongrass cuttings that grew robustly in our community verge garden. This salad is full of lemongrass goodness and fond memories.

VG | SERVES 4~6

21 oz (600 g) firm tofu, cut into 1 in (2 cm)
   cubes
½ lb (200 g) mung bean vermicelli, soaked
   in warm water for 10 minutes
2–3 tablespoons vegetable oil
1 small onion, halved and finely sliced
1 lb (400 g) mixed Asian greens (bok choy,
   choy sum, and Chinese broccoli),
   cut into 2 in (5 cm) pieces
2 cups Asian herb leaves (Thai basil,
   cilantro, green onion, Vietnamese mint,
   or shiso leaves), finely sliced
1–2 tablespoons extra-virgin olive oil
½ cup roasted peanuts, roughly chopped
Sea salt and white pepper

LEMONGRASS MARINADE

4 lemongrass stalks, white parts only,
   very finely chopped
1 garlic clove, very finely chopped
3 tablespoons kecap manis
1 tablespoon soy sauce
½ teaspoon red chili flakes
1 teaspoon ground turmeric
1 teaspoon superfine sugar
Pinch of sea salt

OPTION

For gluten free, use tamari in place
   of soy sauce

For the lemongrass marinade, combine all the ingredients in a bowl and whisk together. The marinade can be made the day before and kept in the fridge until ready to use.

Add the tofu cubes to the marinade, turning to coat evenly, and leave to marinate in the fridge for at least 30 minutes.

When ready to cook, put the vermicelli in a large bowl, and soak in warm water for 10 minutes. Drain, return to the bowl, and season with a big pinch of salt, then pour over enough boiling water to cover and leave for 10–20 seconds to soften fully. Drain immediately and rinse under cold water.

In a large frying pan, heat the vegetable oil and add the onion. Stir-fry the onion for 3–4 minutes until soft, then remove from the pan and set aside. Add the tofu to the pan along with the marinade and cook, moving the tofu pieces around with chopsticks or tongs, until golden brown all over. Return the onion to the pan along with the Asian greens and stir-fry for a further 1–2 minutes, until the greens are wilted.

Combine the tofu and greens with the mung bean vermicelli and herbs and drizzle over the olive oil. Toss together well, season with salt and white pepper, and scatter over the peanuts to serve.

THIS IS AUSTRALIA

Modern Australia is a vibrant mix of cultures from all over the globe. Indeed, this interweaving of influences and experiences is precisely what makes Australia "the lucky country." The Australian table is where food from many different backgrounds and traditions is welcomed and celebrated. Aussie cuisine is light, fresh, and always innovative, inspired by our cosmopolitan cities, golden beaches, rugged bush, and blended history. The salads inspired by the Australia of today can also be identified as Modern Asian, Asian Fusion, Mediterranean-Inspired, New Middle-Eastern, Contemporary British, or Nouveau French. This is culinary pluralism at its best—this is Australia.

TARATOR CAULIFLOWER WITH RAINBOW CHARD AND BULGUR WHEAT

My good friend Elham Abi-Ghanem is a neighborhood treasure. Elham was born in Senegal, of Lebanese descent, and now resides in inner city Sydney where she shares her vast knowledge and love of food with the kids at Bourke Street Public School (where she has volunteered and run the canteen for over 20 years). I have been lucky enough to learn a lot from Elham—she taught me all about this lemony Lebanese tarator, which I have classically teamed with cauliflower and chard (including the stalks!).

VG | SERVES 4~6

1 large cauliflower head (about 2 lb; 1 kg), cut into florets
5–6 tablespoons extra-virgin olive oil
1 small onion, finely diced
1 garlic clove, finely chopped
1½ cups (200 g) bulgur wheat (cracked wheat)
1½ cups (375 ml) vegetable stock
½ bunch (200 g) rainbow chard (about 7 oz; 200 g), leaves and stalks separated
½ cup flat-leaf parsley leaves, roughly chopped
Juice of ½ lemon
½ cup slivered almonds, toasted
Sea salt and black pepper

TARATOR

2 cups (270 g) tahini paste
1 garlic clove, very finely chopped
Juice of 1 large lemon, plus extra if necessary
3 tablespoons finely chopped flat-leaf parsley leaves
Sea salt and black pepper

SUBSTITUTES/OPTIONS

Rainbow chard: spinach, kale, cavolo nero
For gluten free, use quinoa in place of bulgur wheat

Preheat the oven to 400°F (200°C).

Make the tarator by mixing together the tahini, garlic, and lemon juice. Gradually stir in 5 tablespoons of water, a little at a time, until you have a smooth, creamy sauce. You want the consistency of cream. Taste and add a little more lemon juice, if you like, then stir in the parsley and season with salt and lots of pepper.

Place the cauliflower florets on a large baking tray and pour over two-thirds of the tarator, keeping some aside for serving. Drizzle over 1–2 tablespoons of olive oil and mix everything well to coat. Season with salt and pepper and roast for 20–25 minutes until golden.

Heat 2 tablespoons of olive oil in a saucepan over a low heat, add the onion, and sauté for 1 minute until softened. Add the garlic and bulgur wheat and stir well to coat the grains in the oil. Pour over the stock, cover with a lid, bring to a simmer, and cook for 10 minutes, or until the stock has been absorbed and the grains are tender. Remove from the heat, place a clean tea towel over the pan, and leave to sit for 10 minutes to allow the grains to fluff up.

Finely slice the rainbow chard leaves and stalks, keeping them separate. In a frying pan, heat 1 tablespoon of olive oil, add the chard stalks and sauté for 3–4 minutes over medium heat until tender. Add the chard leaves and sauté for another 2 minutes until the leaves are wilted and the stalks are cooked through.

Combine the rainbow chard, bulgur wheat, roasted cauliflower, and parsley. Spoon over the remaining tarator, drizzle over a little olive oil, and squeeze over the lemon juice. Serve topped with the toasted almonds.

BASIL-LEMON SCENTED MILLET
WITH ROASTED BROCCOLI

Millet is an ancient grain with big health benefits—it is rich in iron, B vitamins, and calcium and is a perfect naturally gluten-free alternative to couscous or barley. As a younger vegetarian, I often used millet to make burgers and bakes, but lately, I have rediscovered the delicious versatility of this grain in salads. It is fluffy, like rice or quinoa, but has a subtle corn taste and a lovely lightness which pairs wonderfully with herby oils. Here, millet is scented with a light and airy basil-lemon oil that reminds me of the warm evenings and cooling breezes of summer in Sydney.

GF | SERVES 4~6

2 broccoli heads (about 1 kg), cut into florets
2–3 tablespoons extra-virgin olive oil
4 cups (1 liter) vegetable stock or broth, plus
    extra if necessary
2 cups (400 g) millet
1 cup baby arugula leaves
½ cup basil leaves, torn
3 tablespoons roughly chopped flat-leaf
    parsley leaves
2 oz (60 g) parmesan, shaved
3 tablespoons sunflower seeds, toasted
Sea salt and black pepper

BASIL-LEMON OIL

1 garlic clove, very finely chopped
1 cup basil leaves, torn
¾ cup (185 ml) extra-virgin olive oil
3 tablespoons grapeseed oil or other
    neutral oil
Zest and juice of 1 lemon
Sea salt and black pepper

SUBSTITUTES/OPTIONS

Millet: couscous, pearl barley, or quinoa
    (for gluten free)
For vegans, omit parmesan

Preheat the oven to 400°F (200°C).

In a large bowl, coat the broccoli in 1–2 tablespoons of olive oil and season with salt and pepper. Spread the broccoli on a baking tray and roast for 20–25 minutes, until golden and just tender.

To make the basil-lemon oil, put the garlic, basil, and 1 tablespoon of water into the bowl of a food processor and blitz together until you have a green paste. Add the oils and lemon zest and blitz again, gradually squeezing in the lemon juice, and tasting as you go to achieve a balanced, tangy oil. Season well with salt and pepper. Alternatively, pound the ingredients together using a mortar and pestle for a thicker end result.

Bring the vegetable stock to a boil in a large saucepan. Add the millet, cover with a lid, and simmer over a low heat until all the stock has been absorbed and the grains are tender. (Add more stock or water if you need to, as some brands of millet take longer to cook than others.) Turn off the heat, remove the lid, and leave the millet to sit for 10 minutes to allow the grains to dry out further and fluff up. Once cool, add the basil-lemon oil to the millet and mix well.

To serve, combine the broccoli with the millet, arugula, and herbs, and season with salt and pepper. Drizzle with olive oil and top with the shaved parmesan and sunflower seeds.

GREEN AND GOLD SALAD OF ASPARAGUS AND GOLDEN BEETS WITH FARRO, CRISPY SAGE, AND LEMON BROWN BUTTER

While bursting with hues of green and gold, the colors of my native Australia, this dish emphatically embraces the seasonal produce of New York's farmers' markets. In late spring to early summer, it is with great anticipation that we welcome the abundant arrival of sunny golden beets and robust asparagus at local Greenmarkets and organic purveyors. To me, both ingredients absolutely encapsulate the flavor of trans-seasonal nature and earth. The lemon-scented brown butter dressing is something else, taking the classically pleasing combination of burnt butter and sage on a grand adventure.

SERVES 4~6

2 cups (350 g) farro, rinsed

1 garlic clove, crushed

4 large golden beets (about 2 lb; 1 kg), peeled and cut into thin wedges

3–4 tablespoons extra-virgin olive oil

1 lb (400 g) asparagus, trimmed and cut into 1 in (2.5 cm) pieces

1 cup microgreen sprouts (optional)

1 cup walnuts, toasted

Sea salt and black pepper

LEMON BROWN BUTTER

½ cup (1 stick; 120 g) unsalted butter

½ cup sage leaves

Juice of ½ lemon

1 small garlic clove, very finely chopped

¾ teaspoon dijon mustard

1 teaspoon maple syrup

Sea salt

SUBSTITUTES

golden beets: red or target beets

Preheat the oven to 400°F (200°C).

Add the farro and crushed garlic to a saucepan of boiling salted water and cook for 20 minutes, or until tender. Drain.

Place the beets on a large baking tray, drizzle over 1–2 tablespoons of olive oil, and season with salt. Roast for 25–30 minutes until tender.

Heat 1 tablespoon of olive oil in a large frying pan. Add the asparagus and cook for 1½–2 minutes until just tender but still bright green in color.

To make the lemon brown butter, melt the butter in a small saucepan over medium heat. Add the sage leaves and swirl around in the butter until they begin to crisp, then remove them from the pan, sprinkle over a little salt, and leave to drain on absorbent paper towel. Continue to heat the butter until it is browned and smells nutty, then remove from the heat and leave to cool slightly. Carefully whisk in the lemon juice, garlic, mustard, and maple syrup and add a pinch of salt.

Combine the farro, beets, and asparagus, drizzle over a little olive oil, and season well with salt and pepper. Arrange on a large serving dish and spoon over the lemon brown butter. To serve, scatter over the sprouts, if you like, and the crispy sage leaves and walnuts.

ROASTED SWEET POTATO WITH LEEKS
AND MUSTARD CROUTONS

This salad is a twist on classic potato and leek soup—such an effortless, comforting combination. I've shaken up this classic just a little with the use of sweet potatoes and the addition of buttery mustard croutons and a creamy mustard dressing. And I'll let you in on a little tip—sometimes I do strange things in the kitchen, like blitz up leftover salads into soups (read about it on page 26)! I did just that with this salad (without the croutons) and I can attest that sweet potato and leek makes a rather nice soup too!

SERVES 4~6

6 sweet potatoes (about 3 lb; 1.4 kg),
  unpeeled, washed and cut into ½ in
  (1 cm) cubes
4 small leeks, white and light green parts
  only, finely sliced into rounds and washed
2–3 tablespoons extra-virgin olive oil
3 tablespoons finely chopped chives
2 cups baby arugula leaves
Sea salt and black pepper

MUSTARD CROUTONS

7 tablespoons (100 g) salted butter
2 tablespoons dijon mustard
1 teaspoon thyme leaves
3 teaspoons finely chopped flat-leaf
  parsley leaves
½ lb (250 g) stale bread, such as sourdough
  or ciabatta, torn into 1 in (2 cm) chunks
1 oz (30 g) parmesan, grated
Sea salt and black pepper

MUSTARD DRESSING

1 cup (250 g) Greek yogurt
1½ tablespoons dijon mustard
2 tablespoons extra-virgin olive oil
1 garlic clove, grated
Sea salt and black pepper

Preheat the oven to 400°F (200°C).

For the mustard croutons, melt the butter in a saucepan over a medium heat until it starts to foam. Whisk in the mustard, herbs, and a big pinch of salt and pepper, take off the heat, and leave to cool for a few minutes. Spread the bread pieces out on a large baking tray, pour over the mustard butter and sprinkle over the grated cheese. Mix everything together well to ensure the bread is evenly coated. Bake for about 15 minutes or until the croutons are golden. Set aside to cool.

Arrange the sweet potato and leeks on a large baking tray. Drizzle over 1–2 tablespoons of olive oil and season with salt and pepper. Roast for 20–25 minutes until the vegetables are soft.

To make the mustard dressing, combine the yogurt, mustard, oil, and garlic. Whisk until smooth. Add a little water if it is too thick —you want the consistency of thickened cream. Season with salt and pepper to taste.

Combine the sweet potato and leeks with the chives, arugula, and mustard croutons. To serve, stir through the dressing, drizzle with olive oil, and season with salt and pepper.

SHAVED ZUCCHINI WITH PEARL COUSCOUS AND CHILI-LEMON RICOTTA

In the early days of Arthur Street Kitchen, I discovered the deliciousness of whipped-up feta paired with zucchini. This salad is Part Two of that original recipe, a variation that sees creamy ricotta laced with chili flakes and lemon zest, served with raw shaved zucchini and luscious balls of pearl couscous. Make room for this salad in your repertoire of family favorites!

SERVES 4~6

2 cups (400 g) pearl couscous
5 zucchini (about 1½ lb; 700 g)
½ cup flat-leaf parsley leaves, roughly chopped
½ cup basil leaves, torn
1–2 tablespoons extra-virgin olive oil
3 tablespoons slivered almonds, toasted
Sea salt and black pepper

CHILI-LEMON RICOTTA

2 cups (500 g) ricotta
1 small garlic clove, very finely chopped
1–2 pinches of red chili flakes
Zest and juice of 1 lemon
2 tablespoons extra-virgin olive oil
½ cup (125 g) sour cream
Sea salt and black pepper

Bring a large saucepan of salted water to a boil. Add the pearl couscous, stir well to prevent the balls from sticking and simmer for 6–8 minutes until the couscous is tender. Drain.

Using a mandoline, food processor, or box grater, shave the zucchini into very thin slices.

To make the chili-lemon ricotta, place the ricotta in a mixing bowl and add the garlic, chili flakes, lemon zest, and lemon juice. Whisk together. Add the olive oil, sour cream, and 1–2 tablespoons of water to loosen up the cheese and give you the consistency of thickened cream. Season liberally with salt and pepper.

Combine the zucchini with the pearl couscous and herbs. Fold through the chili-lemon ricotta, add a final swig of olive oil, and season well with salt and pepper. To serve, scatter over the toasted almonds.

SPICED EGGPLANT AND TOMATO RELISH WITH ROASTED BUTTERNUT SQUASH AND CHICKPEAS

This spiced eggplant and tomato relish is my Christmas gifting staple. Packed into pretty jars, this is the most delicious edible gift, to be enjoyed over the holidays with cheese and crackers. When not gifting, pair this relish with sweet roasted butternut squash and chickpeas for a hearty, vegetable-packed salad. This dish definitely exudes a fancy festive attitude.

VG | GF | SERVES 4~6

1 butternut squash (about 3 lb; 1.4 kg), peeled and cut into 1 in (2 cm) cubes
2 tablespoons extra-virgin olive oil
One and one half 15 oz cans (500 g) chickpeas (about 2 cups), drained
2 cups baby spinach leaves
½ cup mint leaves
½ cup cilantro leaves
3 tablespoons slivered almonds, toasted
Sea salt and black pepper

SPICED EGGPLANT AND TOMATO RELISH

⅓ cup (80 ml) extra-virgin olive oil
2 eggplants (about 1¾ lb; 800 g), peeled and cut into ½ in (1 cm) cubes
1 onion, coarsely chopped
1 tablespoon yellow mustard seeds
1 in (2.5 cm) piece of ginger, peeled and grated
1 long green chili, deseeded and finely chopped
2 garlic cloves, finely chopped
1 tablespoon ground cumin
3 whole cloves
2 teaspoons paprika
½ teaspoon ground turmeric
One 15 oz can (425g) diced tomatoes (about 1 cup)
3 tablespoons apple cider vinegar
½ cup (115 g) superfine sugar
Sea salt

SUBSTITUTES

Butternut squash: any variety of winter squash, sweet potato, cauliflower
Chickpeas: butter beans, lentils

Preheat the oven to 400°F (200°C).

Place the butternut squash on a large baking tray, drizzle with the olive oil, and season with salt and pepper. Roast for 20–25 minutes until golden.

To make the relish, heat the oil in a large non-stick saucepan over high heat. Add half the eggplant to the pan and cook for about 5 minutes, until tender and golden, then remove and set aside. Repeat with the remaining eggplant. Reduce the heat to medium, add the onion to the pan and cook, stirring often, for 3–4 minutes until soft, then add the mustard seeds and cook for about 2 minutes, until the seeds start to pop. Add the ginger, chili, garlic, cumin, cloves, paprika, turmeric, and a large pinch of salt and cook for a further 2 minutes. Return the eggplant to the pan along with the tomatoes, vinegar, sugar, and ½ cup (125 ml) of water. Reduce the heat to low, cover with a lid and simmer, stirring occasionally, for 15–20 minutes until the mixture thickens and the eggplant is very soft.

Combine the squash, chickpeas, and baby spinach, and spoon over the relish. Mix everything together well, then scatter over the herbs and slivered almonds to serve.

FRIED BUTTER BEANS AND PEARL BARLEY WITH BABY SPINACH AND CHILI-HERB YOGURT

This recipe goes to show how being well stocked with a few larder basics can produce a knockout salad! Canned legumes, spices, some dried grains, a few fridge greens, and a tub of yogurt can give you this super tasty dish. As always, substitute where needed—chickpeas also work well here, while you can use any grain or cereal you have on hand such as quinoa, freekeh, or spelt.

SERVES 4~6

1½ cups (300 g) pearl barley, rinsed
3–4 tablespoons extra-virgin olive oil
1 garlic clove, very finely chopped
1 teaspoon ground cumin
2 teaspoons ground coriander
1 teaspoon paprika
One and one half 15 oz cans (500 g) butter
    beans (about 2 cups), drained
½ cup flat-leaf parsley leaves (or other soft
    herb), finely chopped
3 cups baby spinach leaves
Juice of ½ lemon
Sea salt and black pepper

CHILI-HERB YOGURT

1 long green or red chili
2 cups (500 g) Greek yogurt
1 small garlic clove, very finely chopped
1 tablespoon chopped mint, dill or
    parsley leaves
2 tablespoons extra-virgin olive oil
Squeeze of lemon juice
Sea salt and black pepper

Place the pearl barley in a large saucepan with plenty of salted water. Bring to a boil and simmer for 30–35 minutes until the barley is tender but retains a chewy bite. Drain.

Heat 1–2 tablespoons of olive oil in a large frying pan over a medium-high heat and add the garlic, cumin, coriander, and paprika. Fry for 30 seconds until the spices are fragrant, then add the drained butter beans and season with a generous amount of salt and pepper. Stir to coat the beans in the spices and fry until the beans are crisp and golden, shaking the pan every now and then to move the beans around and adding more olive oil as needed. Set aside.

To make the chili-herb yogurt, halve the chili, reserving the seeds for later, and finely chop the flesh. Combine the yogurt with the garlic, chili, herbs, olive oil, and lemon juice. Season with salt and pepper to taste. If you would like the yogurt hotter, add some of the reserved chili seeds.

Combine the pearl barley with the parsley, baby spinach, and fried butter beans and drizzle with olive oil. Season with salt and pepper and mix well. To serve, spread the chili-herb yogurt across a large serving platter. Spoon the bean and barley mixture on top of the yogurt and squeeze over the lemon juice to finish.

BLACK-EYED PEAS WITH KALE, FENNEL, CHERRY TOMATOES, AND FENNEL SEED OIL

As a kid, I was fascinated by my mother's secret pantry, full of the exotic ingredients she used in her medicinal broths. Among the ginseng and mystery jars of horns, antlers, and bones, there always sat a bottle of black-eyed peas. So for me, this salad definitely packs a medicinal punch—a simple dish of wholesome black-eyed peas, teamed with nutrient-rich kale, fennel, tomatoes, and a surprising fennel seed oil.

VG | GF | SERVES 4~6

400 g dried black-eyed peas, rinsed
2 garlic cloves, crushed with a heavy knife
1 tablespoon olive oil
½ bunch of kale leaves, washed thoroughly, central stems removed, leaves torn
2 fennel bulbs (about 1¾ lb; 800 g)
½ lb (200 g) cherry tomatoes
½ cup basil leaves
3 tablespoons sunflower seeds, toasted
Sea salt and black pepper

FENNEL SEED OIL

1 tablespoon fennel seeds
1 garlic clove
½ cup basil leaves
1 teaspoon sea salt
½ cup (120 ml) extra-virgin olive oil
Zest of ½ lemon
Black pepper

SUBSTITUTES

Dried black-eyed peas: canned black-eyed peas
Cherry tomatoes: any other tomato variety, diced

Place the black-eyed peas in a saucepan with one of the garlic cloves, cover with water, and bring to a boil. Add a large pinch of salt, reduce the heat to medium, and simmer, covered, for 30–35 minutes until the peas are tender but still holding their shape. Drain and leave to cool, then break up the garlic with the back of a fork and stir through the peas.

For the fennel seed oil, add the fennel seeds to a small frying pan over medium heat and toast for 60 seconds, or until the seeds start to pop and smell aromatic. Tip the toasted seeds into a mortar and pound with a pestle, then add the garlic, basil, and salt and pound to a rough paste. Stir in the olive oil and lemon zest and season with pepper.

Heat the olive oil in a frying pan, add the kale, remaining crushed garlic, and a pinch of salt, and cook over medium heat for 2–3 minutes until the kale is wilted.

Finely slice the fennel with a mandoline, food processor, or sharp knife. Roughly chop the tomatoes.

Combine the black-eyed peas with the kale, fennel, tomatoes and basil. Pour the fennel seed oil over and toss together. For maximum flavor, let this salad sit and marinate for 30 minutes to enable the flavors to come together. When ready to eat, scatter over the sunflower seeds.

BEER-MARINATED MUSHROOMS WITH GREEN LENTILS AND FREEKEH

My former neighborhood of Surry Hills was a creative hub. On Arthur Street where I lived and worked, we were ethical fashion designers, candle-makers, rug-makers, salad-makers, craft beer brewers, and more. Our street corners were our meeting rooms, where we would laugh, chat, and brainstorm. This salad was conceived around the corner on Bourke Street, when I ran into my neighbor Matt King, one third of local brewer The Grifter Brewing Co. The Grifter make rich, full-flavored hand-crafted ales and I wondered how one of their beers would taste in a salad. So this wacky little marriage of beer and mushrooms was born. Use whichever ale you like, making sure it's full-bodied and delicious.

SERVES 4~6

1 oz (30 g) dried porcini mushrooms
1½ lb (750 g) button mushrooms, cleaned
1 cup (200 g) green lentils, rinsed
1 cup (200 g) freekeh, rinsed
1–2 tablespoons extra-virgin olive oil
1 garlic clove, finely chopped
2 teaspoons finely chopped rosemary leaves
1½ tablespoons (20 g) salted butter
1 cup baby spinach leaves
3 tablespoons roughly chopped
   flat-leaf parsley leaves
3 tablespoons finely sliced chives
Juice of ½ lemon
5 oz (150 g) fresh ricotta, crumbled
Sea salt and black pepper

BEER MARINADE

3 cups (700 ml) ale
⅔ cup (150 ml) orange juice
1 in (2.5 cm) piece of ginger, peeled and
   finely chopped
1 long red chili, deseeded and finely
   chopped
2 shallots (see note page 32), finely sliced
2 tablespoons honey
⅓ cup (80 ml) extra-virgin olive oil
2 teaspoons sea salt

SUBSTITUTES

Button mushrooms: any variety of
   mushrooms

Place the porcini mushrooms in a bowl, cover with hot water, and leave to soak for 10 minutes. Remove the porcini mushrooms from the soaking liquid, squeeze out any excess liquid with your hands, and set aside. Reserve a few tablespoons of the mushroom soaking liquid, being sure to avoid the grit at the bottom of the bowl, and discard the rest.

For the beer marinade, combine all the ingredients in a large bowl together with the reserved mushroom soaking liquid and mix well. Add the button and porcini mushrooms to the marinade and leave to marinate in the refrigerator for at least 1 hour, preferably overnight.

Add the lentils and freekeh to a saucepan of salted water. Bring to a boil and cook for 20–25 minutes until both are just tender. Drain and set aside.

Heat 1 tablespoon of olive oil in a large frying pan, throw in the garlic and rosemary, then add the mushrooms and a few tablespoons of the marinade, and fry until the mushrooms are golden (you may have to do this in batches). Remove from the heat and add the butter.

Combine the mushrooms, lentils, freekeh, spinach, parsley, and chives. Drizzle over some olive oil, squeeze over the lemon, and spoon over a little more of the beer marinade. To serve, scatter over the ricotta and season with salt and pepper.

HOMEMADE PANEER WITH LIME-PICKLED CAULIFLOWER AND BLACK-EYED PEAS

The wonderful thing about neighborhoods is the wealth of knowledge gained from transient sidewalk chats, at school drop off, or at the local park. This recipe is rooted in a cauliflower salad recipe from my Surry Hills neighborhood friend Gayu Mudaliar. Her clever and simple Indian-style dish was the inspiration for this whole-hearted salad, complete with homemade paneer and lashings of lime juice. Paneer is really easy to make—all you need is milk and lemon juice. Eat this creamy, mild cheese straight away. And since it doesn't melt, it is robust enough to use in curries and salads, like I have here.

GF | SERVES 4~6

1 cauliflower head (about 1½ lb; 750 g),
　　cut into small florets
Juice of 4 limes
3–4 tablespoons extra-virgin olive oil
2 teaspoons cumin seeds
1 small garlic clove, very finely chopped
One and one half 15 oz cans (500 g)
　　black-eyed peas (about 2 cups), drained
1 long green chili, deseeded and
　　finely chopped
1 in (2 cm) piece of ginger, peeled and
　　finely chopped
3 tablespoons black sesame seeds
3 tablespoons white sesame seeds, toasted
2 tablespoons nigella seeds
½ cup cilantro leaves
Sea salt and black pepper

PANEER

1 gallon (4 liters) full-cream milk
Juice of 2 lemons (about ½ cup; 120 ml),
　　plus extra if necessary

SUBSTITUTES

Homemade paneer: store-bought paneer
Black-eyed peas: chickpeas

Place the cauliflower florets in a ceramic bowl (or other non-reactive bowl) and add half the lime juice and 2 teaspoons of salt. Cover and leave to pickle for at least 2 hours, but the longer the better. You can even leave it to pickle overnight in the refrigerator.

Line a colander with a clean muslin cloth or thin cotton material. To make the paneer, heat the milk in a large saucepan and bring to a slow boil. When the milk starts to rise, stir in the lemon juice. Keep stirring until the milk splits (add more lemon juice if you need to)—eventually, the solid curds will separate from the watery whey. Remove from the heat and pour into the muslin-lined colander to drain off the whey. Press the curd together to form the paneer, rinse in cold water, and fold up the sides of the muslin to form a little bundle. Leave in the colander, put a weight over the top (like a bowl filled with water), and leave it to drain for about 15 minutes.

In a small frying pan, add 2 tablespoons of olive oil and when hot, fry the cumin seeds and garlic for a minute or so, until fragrant. Immediately pour over the cauliflower and mix well.

Crumble up the paneer with your fingers and scatter over the cauliflower. Add the black-eyed peas, remaining lime juice, a drizzle of olive oil, green chili, ginger, and a big pinch of salt. Mix well. To serve, scatter over the black and white sesame seeds, nigella seeds, and cilantro leaves.

CHARGRILLED BROCCOLI RABE AND BELGIAN ENDIVE WITH ROMAINE LETTUCE, WALNUTS, AND STILTON CREAM

One of the truly wonderful things about food is its innate ability to invoke memories and taste-induced nostalgia. When I eat broccoli and Stilton soup, I am instantly transported to a little thatched-roof English pub in the countryside. This salad is a homage to this memory but is somehow less English alehouse and more modern Australian beer garden. It pairs broccoli rabe, or rapini as it is commonly known in some parts of the world, with a creamy, smooth yet punchy Stilton cream. This salad is one of contrasts, with the slight bitterness of the broccoli rabe, Belgian endive, and walnuts beautifully tempered by the creamy dressing.

GF | SERVES 4~6

2¼ lb (1 kg) broccoli rabe, trimmed and
    cut into 2 in (5 cm) pieces
2 Belgian endive (about ½ lb; 220 g),
    trimmed and cut into thin wedges
1–2 tablespoons extra-virgin olive oil
1 romaine lettuce (about 1 lb; 500 g), halved
    lengthways and roughly sliced into
    thick segments
3 tablespoons finely chopped chives
1 cup walnuts, toasted and crushed
Sea salt and black pepper

STILTON CREAM

1 tablespoon extra-virgin olive oil
1 garlic clove
½ cup (125 g) crème fraîche or
    light sour cream
7 oz (200 g) Stilton, crumbled
Pinch of ground nutmeg
1 tablespoon finely chopped chives
Black pepper

SUBSTITUTES

Broccoli rabe: broccoli, broccolini
Stilton: another creamy, soft blue cheese
    like Gorgonzola

Preheat a griddle pan or barbecue to high.

Lightly coat the broccoli rabe and Belgian endive with the olive oil and season with salt. Place the broccoli rabe on the pan or barbecue and cook until slightly charred on each side. Continue until all the broccoli rabe is cooked. Then add the endive wedges and cook for only 30 seconds per side, just enough to soften and get some char marks on the leaves. You don't want them wilted.

To make the Stilton cream, add the olive oil and garlic to a small saucepan and cook for 10 seconds. Pour in the crème fraîche and heat on low heat. Add the Stilton and stir to melt the cheese. Stir in the nutmeg and chives and finish with lots of pepper.

Arrange the romaine lettuce on a large plate or serving board. Place the broccoli rabe and endive on top and sprinkle over the chives and toasted walnuts. Spoon over the Stilton cream and season lightly with pepper.

JUST BRING DESSERT

Like salads, there is something deeply social and inclusive about desserts. Embracing this collaborative spirit, this chapter is written with a little help from my friends. The sweet-makers in this chapter hail from three different continents and have generously shared their ultimate "just bring dessert" recipes that they love to make and take to a social gathering.

These show-stopping-yet-simple recipes are delivered to us with an honest passion, against the backdrop of charming stories and memories of food, family, and friendship.

Hetty McKinnon

CARROLL GARDENS, BROOKLYN (USA)

Hetty will be bringing

SALTED CARAMEL AND APPLE GALETTES

As many of you may know, my career in food started with baking French macarons for a local cafe (owned by my dear friends Remy and Lee) in Surry Hills, Sydney. In those days, I relentlessly chased perfection in my baking. Batches upon batches of imperfect macarons were discarded. I soon learned that making macarons in a non-temperature-controlled home kitchen, amid the humidity of Sydney was not exactly ideal. That career was never going to last.

Still, my short-lived macaron-making business taught me a lot about flavor combinations. It was while making macarons that I discovered the wonders of salt and caramel. My love of this flavor combination led me to this new classic, an incredibly indulgent dessert of fresh seasonal apples laced in salted caramel, wrapped in an incredibly crumbly pie pastry.

These galettes are made in three parts. First, there is the shortcrust, which I have brazenly coined the "best-ever." I am willing to go out on a limb here and back my claim 100 percent. I have made this crust many times and on every occasion it has turned out flaky, melty, and delicious. The best thing of all, you don't need any apparatus to make it, just your fingertips! Next, there is the filling, which is simply apple and spices. The last (but not least) component is the salted caramel—this caramel recipe is super easy and fairly fail-proof, but you do have to exercise caution when you add in the butter and cream as it bubbles quite violently!

SALTED CARAMEL AND APPLE GALETTES

This quantity of pastry is enough to make a traditional 9 in (22 cm) double crust apple pie. If making a pie, just halve the pastry before you chill it—roll out one half for the bottom of the pie, then use the other half for the pie top. For these galettes, I used golden delicious apples, but use whichever apples you have on hand, or even two different varieties. If you have any salted caramel remaining after making the galettes, you can store this in an airtight container in the fridge for 2 weeks (just warm it up before you use it!).

MAKES 6 INDIVIDUAL GALETTES

BEST-EVER SHORTCRUST PASTRY

2 cups (300 g) all-purpose flour, plus extra
    for rolling
3 tablespoons superfine sugar
1 teaspoon salt
¾ cup (1½ sticks; 175 g) cold unsalted butter
½ cup (125 ml) cold full-cream milk, plus
    extra for glazing

FILLING

2–3 apples (about 1 lb; 400 g), peeled
Juice of 1 lemon
2 tablespoons soft brown sugar
¾ teaspoon ground cinnamon
Small pinch of ground nutmeg
½ teaspoon vanilla extract

SALTED CARAMEL

½ cup (115 g) superfine sugar
4 tablespoons (50 g) salted butter
3 tablespoons pouring cream
2 teaspoons sea salt, plus extra
    for sprinkling

To make the pastry, add the flour, sugar, salt, and cold butter to a large bowl. Using your fingertips, work the butter into the flour, until you get pea-sized pieces. You don't need to work it too much at this point. If you still see little blobs of butter, that is fine—it will all add to the melt-in-your-mouth quality of the pastry. Add the cold milk and mix until a dough forms. Do not over mix. The less you work the dough at this point, the flakier (or to use the pastry term, short) your dough will be. Wrap the dough in plastic wrap and leave to rest for at least 1 hour in the refrigerator (or even overnight!).

Note: Keeping your pastry as cold as possible means that the fat won't melt before baking. When the lumps of fat melt in the oven as the pastry bakes, it results in lots of flaky layers and extra deliciousness!

For the filling, if you have an apple corer, core the apples. Using a mandoline or very sharp knife, finely slice the apples all the way through the center so you get nice round slices. If you don't have an apple corer, slice the apples first, then use a sharp paring knife to dig out the cores. Place the apple slices in a bowl and squeeze over the lemon juice to prevent browning and to add flavor. Next, add the brown sugar, cinnamon, nutmeg, and vanilla.

To make the salted caramel, heat the sugar in a saucepan with 2 tablespoons of water. Stir constantly for 4–5 minutes with a wooden spoon or heat resistant rubber spatula. The sugar will eventually melt and turn into an amber-colored liquid. At this point, very carefully add the butter to the sugar mixture and stir until melted. The mixture will bubble as the butter melts. Finally, slowly pour in the cream, taking great care, as the hot mixture will rise in the pan and bubble quite rapidly at this point. Once combined, remove from the heat and add the sea salt.

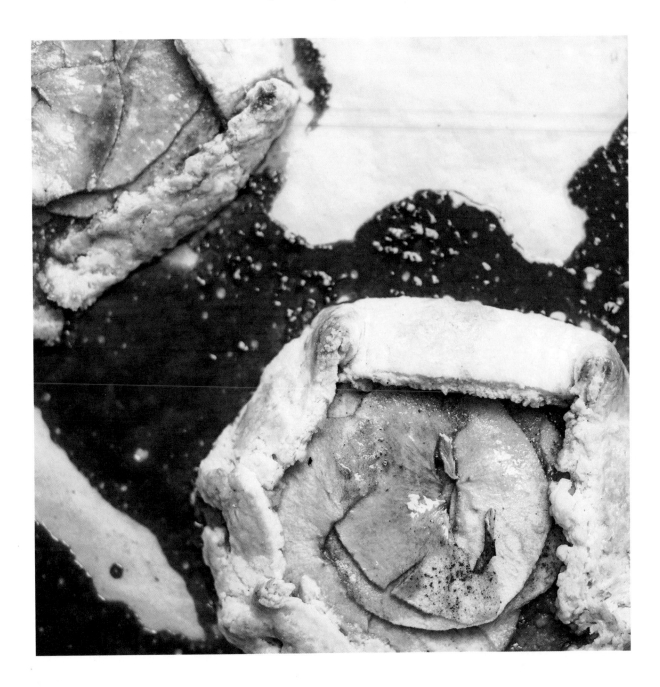

Preheat the oven to 350°F (180°C). Line a baking tray with parchment paper.

Flour your surface and roll out your cold pastry until it is about ¹/₁₀ in (3 mm) thick. Using a plate or bowl, carefully cut out 6 rounds—my pastry rounds measured 6 in (16 cm) each. Transfer the pastry rounds onto the lined baking tray and spread about 2 teaspoons of salted caramel in the middle of

each round, leaving a 1 in (2.5 cm) border around the outside. Sprinkle a few sea salt flakes over the caramel. Pile the apples on top of the caramel, then fold the pastry edges over the apples, pleating to hold the fruit in. Add an extra dollop of salted caramel to the exposed fruit. Brush the pastry with milk and bake in the oven for 30–35 minutes, until it is golden.

Best eaten with vanilla ice cream!

Hetty will also be bringing

SLICE, THREE WAYS

I adore the simplicity and charm of an old-fashioned country slice. To me, it is a very Australian dessert, reminiscent of traditional school fetes or country fairs. Super simple to make, thrown together with pantry ingredients, a slice is my perfect accompaniment to a cup of tea.

I have been making slices to go with salads since the very beginning of Arthur Street Kitchen. A slice is a perfect vice to a salad's virtue. Over the years, I have developed a number of tasty slices that are essentially variations of the one basic recipe.

Each slice starts with a biscuit base, layered with a sweet filling of either caramel, curd, or fruit and topped with either chocolate or toasted coconut. If you are looking for a knockout, absolute beginner, fail-safe sweet recipe, this is it!

FIRST WAY | *LEMON CURD AND COCONUT SLICE*

MAKES ABOUT 20 SQUARES

SLICE BASE

1 cup (90 g) desiccated coconut

1 cup (230 g) soft brown sugar

1 cup (150 g) self-rising flour

½ cup plus 1 teaspoon (125 g) salted butter,
    melted

**LEMON CURD
(MAKES ABOUT 1 CUP/375 G)**

3 large eggs

⅓ cup (80 ml) lemon juice, strained

¾ cup (170 g) superfine sugar

4 tablespoons (50 g) unsalted butter, cut
    into small cubes

Zest of 1 lemon (optional)

TOASTED COCONUT TOPPING

2 cups (180 g) desiccated or shredded coconut

½ cup (115 g) superfine sugar

1 egg, beaten

Preheat the oven to 350°F (180°C). Grease and line a 10 x 15 in (25 x 30 cm) lamington tray or brownie pan with parchment paper.

To make the base, combine the coconut, brown sugar, self-rising flour, and melted butter. Press the mixture into the lined tray using the back of a wooden spoon to smooth out the surface. Bake for 8–10 minutes or until the base is a nice golden brown. Leave to cool.

For the lemon curd, put the eggs, lemon juice, and sugar in a stainless steel bowl and mix well. Place this over a saucepan of simmering water and stir constantly until the mixture becomes the consistency of sour cream or hollandaise sauce (this will take about 10 minutes). Take off the heat and strain immediately. While still hot, whisk in the butter and lemon zest (if you are using).

Finally, for the coconut topping, combine the coconut, superfine sugar, and egg, and mix until well combined.

Spread the lemon curd evenly over the base, smoothing it out with the back of a spoon. Scatter the coconut topping evenly over the curd and bake for 5–6 minutes until golden brown. When completely cool, cut into squares. These slices will keep in the fridge for up to 7 days.

SECOND WAY | *GRILLED BANANA AND COCONUT SLICE*

MAKES ABOUT 20 SQUARES

1 x quantity Slice Base (see above)

1 x quantity Toasted Coconut Topping
    (see above)

FILLING

3–4 bananas, sliced lengthways into 3 pieces

1 tablespoon soft brown sugar

One 14 oz can (395 g) sweetened
    condensed milk

3 tablespoons golden syrup or light corn
    syrup

2 tablespoons (30 g) salted butter

Preheat the oven to 350°F (180°C). Grease and line a 10 x 15 in (25 x 30 cm) lamington tray or brownie pan with parchment paper.

Begin by caramelizing the bananas. Heat your grill to a hot setting. Put the banana slices on a baking tray lined with parchment paper and sprinkle over the brown sugar. Place under the hot grill and cook for 3–4 minutes, until the sugar on top starts to caramelize and turn golden. Leave to cool.

Press the slice base mixture into the lined tray, using the back of a wooden spoon to smooth out the surface. Bake for 8–10 minutes, or until the base is a nice golden brown. Leave to cool.

Combine the condensed milk, golden syrup, and butter in a small, heavy-based saucepan and heat gently over medium heat. Stir constantly until the butter melts and the mixture boils (you need to keep stirring, otherwise the mixture will burn on the bottom). Pour onto the base, arrange the caramelized bananas on top, and return to the oven for another 8–10 minutes or until golden.

Spread the coconut topping evenly over the filling and bake for a further 5–6 minutes until golden brown. When completely cool, cut into squares. Slices can be stored in the fridge for up to 7 days.

THIRD WAY | *SALTED CARAMEL AND CHOCOLATE SLICE*

MAKES ABOUT 20 SQUARES

1 x quantity Slice Base (see opposite)

FILLING

One 14 oz can (395 g) sweetened
    condensed milk

⅓ cup (80 ml) golden syrup or light
    corn syrup

4 tablespoons (50 g) salted butter

2–3 teaspoons sea salt (vary according
    to how salty you like it)

TOPPING

7 oz (200 g) dark chocolate, broken into
    pieces

Preheat the oven to 350°F (180°C). Grease and line a 10 x 15 in (25 x 30 cm) lamington tray or brownie pan with parchment paper.

Press the slice base mixture into the lined tray, using the back of a wooden spoon to smooth out the surface. Bake for 8–10 minutes, or until the base is a nice golden brown. Leave to cool.

For the filling, combine the condensed milk, golden syrup, and butter in a small, heavy-based saucepan and heat gently over medium heat. Stir constantly until the butter melts and the mixture comes to a simmer (you need to keep stirring, otherwise the mixture will burn on the bottom). Add your desired amount of salt. Pour onto the base and return to the oven for another 10 minutes or until the caramel is golden and bubbly. Set aside to cool.

To melt the chocolate, place it in a glass or stainless steel bowl. In a saucepan, bring some water to the boil—once boiling, turn off the heat. Immediately put the bowl of chocolate on top of the saucepan and leave it to melt—it should take 8–10 minutes. Once melted (it becomes glossy), stir until smooth.

Pour the melted dark chocolate over the caramel filling, smoothing with a flat spatula.

Once the chocolate has set, you are ready to cut into squares. To make cutting easier, I usually sit a knife in boiling water to heat it up. Once nice and hot, dry it off with a paper towel and cut your slices—having a heated knife will help stop the chocolate from cracking. These slices store in the fridge for at least 7 days.

Jennifer Wong

SURRY HILLS, SYDNEY (AUSTRALIA)

Jennifer will be bringing

CLASSIC PAVLOVA

Jen is one of my oldest friends. We met at university, where we bonded over movie marathons between lectures and seminars. While we both studied the social sciences and media, such are the mysteries of life that somehow I ended up tossing salads and Jen ended up as a really amazing lawyer.

Apart from our mutual love of cinema and, in particular, movies based on young adult fiction, we also share a love of food. Jen and I have attended countless cooking classes together, making everything from mozzarella and pastries to marshmallows, praline, and brioche. There was also one shamefully failed attempt at making nougat, which we don't really talk about anymore (note, I have since rectified said disaster, to the chagrin of my overworked Kitchenaid mixer). I have known Jen to stay up into the wee hours, baking like there is no tomorrow. For every salad I have made, Jen has dished out a killer cake. She really is the sweet to my savory. And while she makes a mean coconut cake and a terrific tiramisu, she is totally the queen of the pavlova, one of my favorite desserts.

For Jen, making pavlova is a labor of love—her recipe was her mother's, which she has now made her own.

"I am known for my pavlova. It is a New Year's favorite with my friends and highly sought after among my coworkers. My original pavlova recipe is contained in my old leather Filofax, quickly jotted down several years ago when talking to my mum on the telephone. I have modified my mum's recipe, experimenting with several versions. A good pav has a crisp outer shell and a creamy, solid meringue filling that, when cut, can hold itself like a slice of cake, even with the weight of the fruit and cream on top. I include cream of tartar, cornstarch, and arrowroot to achieve this, however these ingredients are optional—without them I find that the pavlova is flatter and the meringue center is less firm, but still delicious."

CLASSIC PAVLOVA

My philosophy in regard to pavlova toppings is "never say never." My go-to topping is a layer of thickened cream covered with diced berries (whatever is in season) tossed through passion fruit pulp. In summer I love a layer of mascarpone and a layer of sliced mangoes, topped with toasted coconut.

SERVES 8

6 egg whites
½ teaspoon cream of tartar (optional)
2 cups (460 g) superfine sugar
1 teaspoon vanilla essence (or be adventurous and substitute with rosewater or orange blossom)
2 teaspoons white vinegar
1 tablespoon cornstarch (optional)
2 tablespoons arrowroot (optional)

TO SERVE

1 cup (200 ml) thickened or whipped cream
Seasonal fruit tossed with passion fruit pulp or raspberry coulis

Preheat the oven to 400°F (200°C). Line a baking tray with parchment paper.

In a clean, dry bowl beat the egg whites with an electric mixer on medium-high speed until stiff peaks form. With the mixer still going, add the cream of tartar, if using, and slowly add the sugar a spoon at a time. You need to keep mixing until all the sugar dissolves and the meringue is glossy (I find this takes around 10 minutes).

Reduce the mixer speed to low and fold in the vanilla, white vinegar, and the cornstarch and arrowroot, if using.

Pile the meringue in the middle of the lined baking tray and using a knife (I use my grandmother's old butter knife) make a circle shape with a flat top and smooth sides (like you would ice a cake). The circumference should be the size of a dinner plate. Note: this is where I differ from my mum, she prefers to heap the pav into a rough circle on the baking tray with a slight well in the center.

Place the meringue on the bottom shelf of your oven, shut the door and turn the oven down to 285–300°F (140–150°C). Cook for 70 minutes. The meringue should bake to a warm cream color—if it's starting to look toasty in color, turn the oven temperature down by 10°. At no time during the baking should you open the oven door.

Turn the oven off and leave it to cool completely. To serve, layer with cream and fruit.

Essential pavlova tips from Jennifer:

• The stiffer the egg white, the better the meringue.

• Humidity is meringue's enemy. In humid conditions, your pavlova will be flat.

• Bake it just before you go to bed. The best results come from never opening the oven door. I bake the pav for 1 hour 10 minutes, turn the oven off, and leave it overnight. At a minimum, don't open the oven door until the oven has cooled completely.

• Don't stress if your pavlova cracks, I don't understand people's obsession with avoiding cracks. The best thing about a pavlova is that you cover it with so much cream and fruit, no one cares about a perfect looking shell.

Wesley Verhoeve

CLINTON HILL, BROOKLYN (USA)

Wesley will be bringing

RASPBERRY MOUSSE

Wesley is a modern man. He is a Brooklyn-based photographer, writer, documentarian and multi-disciplinary creative. Through his extraordinary photography project, "One of Many," Wesley travels around the United States, camera in hand, exploring the creative communities of twelve American cities. Since my arrival in his home borough, he has been a great provider of tea and conversation.

Wesley, like myself, confesses to being "not a dessert person." He does, however, have one powerful sweet recipe up his sleeve. I have made this dessert several times already and I can assure you, it is a crowd pleaser. It is also the dessert that my children actually ask for, time and time again.

This raspberry mousse is Wesley's dinner party go-to:

"What I like best about this mousse is that it's visually appealing and it 'feels' impressive for guests, even though it's easy and requires few ingredients. I like making it in front of people, because you only want to prepare it mere minutes before people eat it. Making it is a little bit of a show and then you get the pay-off of watching people eat it right after. The recipe is something my grandmother used to make, as I'm sure many other grandmothers did in their day. To me it feels like a modern classic and I've passed it on to many friends because it's so great for dinner parties and making in volume."

RASPBERRY MOUSSE

Substitute the raspberries with other frozen fruit such as mixed berries, blackberries, or even mangoes.

GF | SERVES 4

10 oz (300 g) frozen raspberries
2–3 tablespoons honey
5 egg whites

TO SERVE (OPTIONAL)

Fresh raspberries
Whipped cream

Place the frozen raspberries in a small food processor or use a hand-held blender and pulse to chop them up, keeping the pieces quite large—you are looking for a rough puree.

Add the honey and pulse a bit more, then add the egg whites and process until it's all fluffy and smooth. The color will have lightened and the volume will have grown. This should only take 2 minutes.

Spoon a big dollop of the mousse into four glasses (like whiskey glasses) and serve immediately, topping each with a puff of whipped cream and some fresh berries, if you like.

Bianca Presto

RADLETT, HERTFORDSHIRE (UK)

Bianca will be bringing

SOUTH AFRICAN MELKTERT (MILK TART)

I met Bianca over a decade ago in London, a day or so after the London bombings of 2005. I was interviewing her for a job. When Bianca turned up for our meeting, she was a little (or a lot) frazzled as she had just lost her mobile phone in the back of a black cab, adding to the sense of panic already pervasive in the air. From that first anxious meeting, I adored her complete lack of pretense and, of course, gave her the job. While we have lived in different cities for most of our friendship, somehow her South African feistiness and my Aussie sarcasm have made us long-time, long-distance mates who bond over a love of homemade bagels and baking adventures.

Bianca grew up in a family of feeders. And eaters, for that matter. During her childhood, Bianca's father ran a restaurant and in later years produced traditional boiled bagels based on a recipe from his great-grandmother.

Bianca remembers: "My first job at fourteen was working as a waitress in a Jewish delicatessen that my father managed at the time. My mother was the family's resident baker; no matter what the occasion, she always had an appropriate cake up her sleeve and my fourteen-year-old self still credits her with my 'Best in Class' Home Economics award after she coached me to greatness with some perfectly formed spinach and gruyere vol-au-vents.

"My early memories of dating my now-husband Steve are steeped in food-related nostalgia. From the first meal I cooked for him in the hostel where we met (grilled chicken pieces dusted with crushed salt and vinegar crisps, an idea from my Granny Sheila) to the very first time I made him his absolute favorite dessert, a milk tart. To give it its proper name, 'melktert' is a traditional South African dessert consisting of sweet pastry crust filled with a creamy cinnamon-infused custard. This recipe was given to me by my mother, it was passed down to her by her grandmother and I think it may have just made my husband finally commit!"

SOUTH AFRICAN MELKTERT (MILK TART)

For ease, or when we're baking with our daughter, we'll use a ready-made puff pastry or pie crust. Equally, this recipe works really well with a base of crushed graham crackers.

MAKES ONE 9 IN (23 CM) TART

2 cups (500 ml) whole milk
1 cinnamon stick
3 tablespoons superfine sugar
3 tablespoons all-purpose flour
1 tablespoon cornstarch
Pinch of salt
3 tablespoons (40 g) salted butter
3 eggs, beaten

PASTRY DOUGH

4 tablespoons (50 g) salted butter
1½ cups (225 g) plain flour,
   plus extra for dusting
⅔ cups (150 ml) pouring cream

TO SERVE

Ground cinnamon
Confectioners' sugar

Prepare your pastry dough ahead of time. In a bowl, rub the butter into the flour with your fingers. Add the cream and mix until a dough forms. Don't over mix. Roll into a flat disc, wrap in plastic wrap, and put it in the fridge to rest for about an hour.

Preheat the oven to 400˚F (200˚C). Grease a shallow, 9 in (23 cm) pie dish with butter (including the edges) and lightly flour.

In a saucepan, boil the milk and cinnamon until it just starts to bubble and rise. In a separate bowl, combine the sugar, flour, cornstarch, and salt. Gradually add the dry ingredients to the hot milk, stirring continuously with a whisk or wooden spoon to prevent lumps. Cook slowly, stirring continuously for 3–5 minutes, until the mixture starts to thicken. Remove from the heat and add the butter. Leave the mixture to cool for a minute or so, then very slowly stir in the eggs (you don't want scrambled eggs!).

On a lightly floured surface, roll out the pastry to a thickness of ⅛ in (3 mm) and use to line the pie dish. Trim off any excess around the edges. Pour in the milk custard mix.

Bake in the oven at 400°F (200°C) for 10 minutes, then reduce the heat to 325°F (160°C) and bake for another 20 minutes until the tart is set. Remove and leave to cool slightly. To serve, dust with cinnamon and confectioners' sugar and enjoy warm, at room temperature, or cold from the fridge.

Samantha Hillman

WILLIAMSBURG, BROOKLYN (USA)

Samantha will be bringing

ORANGE BLOSSOM, YOGURT, AND CARDAMOM CAKE

Originally from the idyllic South Coast of NSW in Australia, Sam Hillman moved to New York as a Jill-Of-All-Food-Trades who successfully maneuvers a career as a recipe developer, food stylist, writer, and content developer.

I will never forget the first time Sam and I shared lunch. It was on one of those snowy days during the coldest February in New York for more than 80 years. As you do, she came to my house bearing a few containers of really delicious cooking stock! As the snow fell vigorously outside, we bunkered down and cooked. I dished up a warming salad of wild mushroom and kasha (the recipe is on page 51). We chatted and laughed. By the time our bellies were full, we both looked outside and the backyard had transformed into a Narnia-esque winter wonderland. An absolutely magical afternoon, inside and out.

Sam is a throw-it-together kind of gal when it comes to baking. She is not afraid to break the rules and try new things and, in this recipe she shares with us, her bravery delivers hugely on flavor, texture, and pure deliciousness.

Sam says, "I came up with this recipe by crossing Donna Hay's yogurt cake with a recipe for Moroccan orange blossom cake. I love to cook it for friends because it's one of those throw-it-all-in-and-give-it-a-stir type scenarios, which is perfect for me because I have the attention span of a three-year-old and refuse to let creaming butter and sugar get in the way of cake and me! I make it for anything, everything, and everyone, but my favorite way to eat it is with my mum, with a pot of tea on the side."

ORANGE BLOSSOM, YOGURT, AND CARDAMOM CAKE

This cake is also amazing made with macadamia oil instead of the butter! It has the same delicious taste, but stays softer for even longer.

SERVES 6-8

1 cup plus 2 tablespoons (250 g) salted
   butter, melted and cooled

2 eggs, beaten

2 teaspoons vanilla extract

Zest of 1 orange

3 tablespoons orange juice

1 cup (250 g) Greek yogurt

2 teaspoons orange blossom water

2 cups (300 g) self-rising flour

1½ cups (330 g) raw granulated sugar

1 teaspoon ground cardamom (or seeds
   from 8–10 cardamom pods, crushed)

2 tablespoons chopped pistachios,
   to decorate

ORANGE AND CREAM CHEESE ICING

4 oz (125 g) cream cheese, at room
   temperature

¾ cup (90 g) confectioners' sugar

Dash of vanilla extract

2 tablespoons orange juice

Preheat the oven to 325°F (160°C). Grease and line a 9 in (22 cm) springform pan with parchment paper.

Begin by combining the wet ingredients. Whisk together the butter, eggs, vanilla extract, orange zest, orange juice, yogurt, and orange blossom water in a bowl.

Combine the flour, sugar, and cardamom and mix well.

Add the flour mixture to the wet ingredients and fold until just combined. Pour into the prepared pan and bake for 50–60 minutes, until a skewer comes out clean. Leave to cool completely.

Prepare the icing by whisking together the cream cheese, confectioners' sugar, vanilla extract, and orange juice. Combine well, until there are no lumps and the icing is smooth in texture.

Spread the icing over the cooled cake and top with the chopped pistachios. Serve immediately.

Ron and Leetal Arazi

BEDFORD-STUYVESANT, BROOKLYN (USA)

Ron and Leetal will be bringing

SHAMISHI

Soon after we arrived in Brooklyn, I received a welcome email from Ron and Leetal Arazi, then strangers to me, offering to show me around my new home borough. A few weeks later, they introduced me to the colorful, bustling Russian neighborhood of Brighton Beach in Brooklyn. So began our food-inspired friendship.

Ron and Leetal are owners of NY Shuk, manufacturers of the tastiest Middle Eastern and North African inspired condiments. They moved to Brooklyn from Israel a few years ago, seeking to introduce New Yorkers to "real" homemade harissa, tanzeya, l'ekama, and other traditional Jewish Sephardic culinary traditions. Ron's handmade couscous is unspeakably good, while pastry chef Leetal effortlessly dishes out the most heavenly desserts.

Leetal shares her family recipe for shamishi: "This is a cake that my grandmother made every year during our family celebration of 'Tu B'Shevat,' a Jewish holiday where you celebrate a 'new year' for the trees. When we moved to NYC and started catering, we wanted to cook foods that authentically represent us. This is how shamishi became our signature dessert! We took the original recipe and gave it the NY Shuk treatment, reducing some of the sweetness that is typical of Middle Eastern desserts. Now, at any special dinner, shamishi cake will be served as the centerpiece. Depending on the season, we pair the cake with different toppings, from citrus fruit in the winter, to strawberry in the summer."

SHAMISHI

This is a rose-scented semolina cake with whipped cream, strawberry sauce, and pistachios.

SERVES 80-100

7 cups (875 g) semolina
1½ cups (90 g) shredded coconut
1¼ cups (250 g) superfine sugar
2 teaspoons baking soda
½ teaspoon baking powder
Pinch of sea salt
1½ cups (375 g) unsalted butter, melted
2 cups (500 g) Greek yogurt
¾ cup (100 g) chopped pistachios,
    to decorate

SUGAR SYRUP

5 cups (1.15 kg) superfine sugar
2 tablespoons honey
Juice from ¾ lemon
5 drops rosewater essence

YOGURT WHIPPED CREAM

2 cups (475 ml) thickened cream
1 tablespoon confectioners' sugar, plus
    extra if necessary
¼ cup (75 g) Greek yogurt
Zest of 1 orange

STRAWBERRY SAUCE

1 lb (450 g) fresh or frozen hulled
    strawberries
1 tablespoon confectioners' sugar, plus extra
    if necessary

IMPORTANT NOTE:

This recipe makes a HUGE shamishi cake
and can be cut into 80–100 2 in (5 cm)
pieces. Hence it is perfect for a big
gathering or party. Otherwise, to make a
more conservative amount, halve the
recipe and use a 11 x 9 in (29 x 24 cm) cake
pan to make 45–50 pieces. Remember to
reduce the cooking time by half if you are
making a smaller version of this recipe.

Preheat the oven to 350°F (180°C). Grease a round 18 in (46 cm) cake pan or a 18 x 13 in (46 x 33 cm) baking sheet with butter.

To make the sugar syrup, place the sugar and honey in a deep saucepan with 5 cups (1.25 liters) of water and bring to a boil over high heat. Make sure to mix so the sugar won't caramelize. Once boiled, lower the heat to medium and continue cooking until the sugar and water thickens to a syrup consistency. A good way of testing for the perfect consistency is to put a few plates in the freezer and place a tablespoon of the syrup on the plate—drag your finger through it to draw a line and, if it stays, the syrup is ready. If the line disappears then cook the syrup a little bit more. Once ready, squeeze in the lemon juice. Leave to cool completely, then stir through the rosewater essence and mix together well. Set aside.

Mix the semolina, coconut, sugar, baking soda, baking powder, and sea salt together in a bowl, add the melted better and mix well using your hands. Once the butter is fully incorporated, add the yogurt and mix. Transfer the cake mixture into the pan and use a spatula to smooth and even out the surface. Score the cake with a knife in a crosshatch pattern to create square- or diamond-shaped pieces that are about 2 in (5 cm) in size. Bake in the oven for 40 minutes, turning the cake around after the first 20 minutes to ensure even baking, until nice and golden. Remove from the oven and pour over the cold syrup. Leave to cool.

For the yogurt cream, whip the cream with the confectioners' sugar until soft peaks form. Gently fold in the yogurt using a spatula, then add the orange zest and give it one more mix. Taste and add more sugar if you like it sweeter.

To make the strawberry sauce, using a hand-held blender, whiz the strawberries together with the sugar until you get a smooth sauce. Taste and add a little more sugar if you like it sweeter.

To serve, spoon 2 tablespoons of the strawberry sauce onto the center of a serving plate. Cut a piece of the cake and place on top, add a dollop of the cream, and sprinkle over a few pistachios.

Jodi Moreno

WEST VILLAGE AND AMAGANSETT, NEW YORK (USA)

Jodi will be bringing

RHUBARB CUSTARD TART WITH A MACADAMIA NUT CRUST AND RASPBERRY ICE

I met Jodi during the first days of spring in New York. She came to my house bearing a bag of sugar snap peas and our friendship was solidified. Jodi is wildly talented and creates mind-blowing gluten-free, dairy-free dishes. She reintroduced me to the joys of long-forgotten grains like millet and at lunch, she serves up crazy good things like horchata, a tropical Mexican drink of almond or rice milk, vanilla, and cinnamon. Nowadays, when I'm looking for healthy food inspiration or just want to spoil myself by looking at pretty pictures, I often find myself digging around Jodi's beautiful blog *What's Cooking Good Looking*. It truly is inspiring.

Jodi has an innate ability to create healthy desserts that taste indulgent. This rhubarb custard tart is a tour de force in gluten-free and dairy-free baking—the recipe is a real eye-opener in how to achieve texture and flavor without automatically reaching for flour and butter.

For Jodi, this sweet is perfect to bring for dessert as it is healthy yet full of wonderful things such as rhubarb: "Rhubarb is best known for being paired with strawberries and made into pie, which also happens to be the only dessert as a child I did not care for. It wasn't until I grew up and started cooking on my own that I became fascinated with rhubarb and all of the wonderful things you could make with it. Now when rhubarb comes along, I cannot get enough. These days, I am always trying to come up with desserts that are dairy- and gluten-free, but equal to or better than their butter and white flour counterparts. This rhubarb tart has become my (personal) most-loved dessert recipe because it naturally achieves that super dessert status by using ingredients that are better for you, but the best part is the vegan rhubarb custard (made possible with coconut milk and agar-agar flakes). It's so delicious, it's hard to not eat it all with a spoon before it makes its way into the tart crust."

NEIGHBORHOOD

RHUBARB CUSTARD TART WITH
A MACADAMIA NUT CRUST AND RASPBERRY ICE

Since rhubarb is super seasonal, you can make this tart using other fruits that are in season. Just sub in the same quantity of whatever fruit you like for the rhubarb.

VG | GF | SERVES 8

CRUST

3 tablespoons shredded coconut

1¼ cups (200 g) macadamia nuts

½ cup (60 g) rolled oats

½ teaspoon sea salt

1 cup (175 g) brown rice flour

3 tablespoons melted coconut oil

1 teaspoon vanilla extract

RHUBARB CUSTARD

7 stalks rhubarb (about 1⅓ cups; 600 g),
   green tops removed and rhubarb chopped

⅔ cup (170 ml) maple syrup

¼ teaspoon ground cinnamon

1 tablespoon vanilla extract
   (or 1 vanilla pod, split and scraped)

1¼ tablespoon lime juice

¼ teaspoon salt

1⅓ cup (330 ml) coconut milk

2 tablespoons agar-agar flakes (or
   2 teaspoons agar-agar powder)

1 tablespoon orange juice

RASPBERRY ICE (OPTIONAL)

1 cup (140 g) frozen raspberries

Preheat the oven to 300°F (150°C). Grease a 9 in (23 cm) tart pan.

Start by making the crust. Spread the coconut out onto a baking sheet and bake for 5 minutes until lightly toasted. Remove from the oven and tip into a food processor. Increase the oven temperature to 350°F (180°C). Add the macadamia nuts, oats, and salt to the coconut in the food processor and pulse many times until you have a very finely ground texture. Transfer to a bowl and add the brown rice flour, melted coconut oil, and vanilla extract, and stir to form a dough. The dough should be wet and should stick together, but should not be too sticky. If it's too sticky, then leave it to sit for a few minutes to dry out slightly.

With clean hands, form the dough into a ball, then place it in the center of the tart pan and press it in with your fingers to mold it to the pan. Poke a few holes in the bottom with a fork, then bake for 20–25 minutes until light brown. Leave the crust to cool for several minutes, then place it in the fridge to completely cool for at least an hour (you can also do this a few days in advance).

To prepare the custard, add the rhubarb, maple syrup, cinnamon, vanilla extract, 1 teaspoon of the lime juice, and the salt to a heavy-based saucepan over medium-low heat. Cook, stirring occasionally, for about 20 minutes, or until the rhubarb is very soft (if it gets too hot and starts bubbling, turn the heat down, as you don't want to burn the rhubarb). Mash the cooked rhubarb with a potato masher to a fairly smooth consistency, add the coconut milk, and stir to incorporate, then stir in the agar-agar flakes and bring to a simmer. Reduce the heat to low, cover, and cook, stirring every few minutes, for 15 minutes, or until the agar-agar has dissolved (just look closely to see if there are any flakes left—if there are, cook for a few minutes more). Remove from the heat and leave the mixture to cool for 10–15 minutes.

Once cooled, transfer the rhubarb mixture to a food processor, add the orange juice and the remaining 1 tablespoon of lime juice, and blend for about 1 minute until the mixture is smooth. Leave the mixture to sit (in the food processor) for 10 minutes. This will allow it to cool and thicken even further. Then blend again until it's super smooth.

To assemble, pour the rhubarb mixture into the chilled tart crust and smooth the top. Place the tart in the fridge and leave to set for at least 2 hours, ideally overnight. (It's best to have patience with this one—if you cut into it too soon, the crust and the inside might fall apart. The longer it sits, the better it will hold together.)

When you're ready to serve, make the raspberry ice (this topping it totally optional). Place the frozen raspberries into the food processor and pulse several times until you have a fine-grain ice. Remove the tart from the fridge, top with the raspberry ice and serve immediately.

Charlotte Ree

GLEBE, SYDNEY (AUSTRALIA)

Charlotte will be bringing

CREAMY RICE WITH CARAMELIZED PEARS

Charlotte loves food. I would almost say she lives and breathes it. When she visited me in New York, I don't think there was a moment when she didn't have an edible item in her mouth, in her hand, or hidden in her bag. She loves to try it all.

While some of her encyclopedic food knowledge may come from her day job as a book publicist talking up cookbooks, her robust food know-how actually stems from first hand experience in the kitchen. Charlotte is a baking goddess—she cooks and eats with abandon and documents these culinary feats on her wonderful blog *Charlotte Eats*, where she dishes up clever treats such as Bacon Brownies, Kingston Biscuits, and Chocolate Peanut Butter Cheesecake. Ultimately, she owes her love of sweet indulgence to the wonderful desserts she grew up eating, including this intergenerational creamy rice recipe, which Charlotte has personalized with caramelized pears.

"My nanny gave this recipe to my mama and my mama gave it to me. We eat it warm in winter and cool in summer, a year round love hug. No matter where I am or whom I am with, making and tasting this recipe immediately transports me back to home. Memories of my nanny and mama stirring the pot on the stove or fighting my brother for the last bowlful, this is my ultimate comfort food."

CREAMY RICE WITH CARAMELIZED PEARS

Creamy rice (or rice pudding as normal folk call it) is a dessert from my childhood and my ultimate comfort food. This particular recipe has been passed down from generation to generation but I have added my own little twist to it—caramelized pears.

GF | SERVES 6, GENEROUSLY

6 cups (1.5 liters) whole milk
1 cup (220 g) arborio rice
½ cup (115 g) demerara sugar,
   or more depending on how much
   sweetness you prefer
1 teaspoon vanilla extract or
   1 vanilla pod, split and scraped
1 cinnamon stick
Ground nutmeg, to serve

CARAMELIZED PEARS

4 tablespoons (60 g) unsalted butter
3 buerre bosc pears, halved
3 tablespoons soft brown sugar
1 teaspoon vanilla extract
Pinch of salt

In a large saucepan, combine the milk, rice, sugar, vanilla, and cinnamon. Slowly bring to the boil, stirring occasionally. Once boiled, turn the heat down to medium-low and stir constantly for 20–25 minutes until the mixture is thick and the rice grains are soft. Take off the heat.

Meanwhile, for the caramelized pears, melt the butter in a large frying pan over medium-high heat. Add the pear pieces, cut-side down, and cook for 4–5 minutes until golden. Mix the sugar together with 1 tablespoon of water and stir to combine. Turn the pears skin-side down, add the sugar and water mixture, and cook until the sauce has thickened slightly. This should take around 2 minutes. Stir in the vanilla extract and salt.

Divide the rice among serving bowls, top each with a pear half, and drizzle over the caramel sauce. Sprinkle over a little nutmeg to finish.

Erika Raxworthy

HIGHBURY, LONDON (UK)

Erika will be bringing

OLIVE OIL AND SEA SALT MOLTEN BROWNIES

Erika Rax, as she is more commonly known, is a natural born creator. As is well documented on her eponymous blog, she is a home baker, plant lover, compulsive crafter, and freelancer, but these labels don't really even touch on the boundless talents of this girl wonder.

While Erika styled the gorgeous photos in this volume with her signature aplomb, she is so much more than a food and prop stylist. Over the years, Erika and I have worked on a few projects together, but my favorite one was when she showed my daughter and her friends how to make their own terrariums. She's just handy like that. Erika is also a rabid baker, with a well-known sweet tooth. On her blog, she lays the sweet on thick with fun and clever recipes like Ginger Caramel Lava Cake, Pretzel Peanut Butter Mini Cheesecakes, Salted Caramel Swirl Marshmallows, and Popsicle Affogato. Erika's perfect sharing dessert, Olive Oil and Sea Salt Molten Brownies, is a fine example of her craftiness in the kitchen:

"I found a recipe for cookies online that somewhat fit what ingredients I had in the pantry. After my adaptations, I realized that the batter was more suited to a cake. It later evolved into a brownie after I put it in the fridge and it became super fudgy.

"It's now my go-to recipe if someone is coming over or if I just need something chocolatey. I almost always use a different kind of chocolate to stir through (white chocolate or a whole hazelnut chocolate is amazing), which makes it different every time."

NEIGHBORHOOD

OLIVE OIL AND SEA SALT MOLTEN BROWNIES

This molten brownie is incredibly adaptable. Add in whatever half-eaten chocolate bars you have lying around in your pantry. In the brownie pictured opposite, I used a chocolate bar with peanut butter and pretzels—and it was so good!

SERVES 9-12

2 eggs
1 cup (230 g) dark brown sugar
½ cup (125 ml) extra-virgin olive oil
1 teaspoon vanilla extract
¾ cup (110 g) self-rising flour
¾ cup (90 g) cocoa powder, sifted
1 teaspoon coarse sea salt flakes
3½ oz (100 g) chocolate, roughly chopped
   (any type will do: white, milk, dark)

Preheat the oven to 350°F (180°C). Grease and line a 9 in (22 cm) square cake pan.

In a bowl, whisk together the eggs, sugar, olive oil, and vanilla extract until mixed well. Add the flour, cocoa, and salt, and stir well to form a thick but smooth batter, then stir through the chocolate bits.

Pour the mixture into the prepared pan and bake for about 10 minutes. The center should still be a little bit wobbly, but not liquid—poke it with your finger and if it feels set but still soft, then it's done. Don't over-bake!

Cool on a wire rack and cut into squares or rectangular slices to serve—the size of your slice is up to you! Serve slightly warm or leave in the fridge overnight and slice for super fudgy brownies. Brownies can be stored in the fridge for up to 7 days.

ACKNOWLEDGMENTS

I began writing this book during the winter in New York City, after two months on the road in Europe, feeling inspired by family, food and life. While writing is often a solitary act, there were many people in those early snowy months in New York who provided me with friendship, who cooked with me, or made me tea. Thank you to Jodi Moreno, Ron and Leetal Arazi, Wesley Verhoeve, Karen Mordechai, and Samantha Hillman for giving me an experience of writing that felt extremely social.

When I think of the people who have changed the course of my life, Luisa Brimble is at the top of that list. Thank you for being extraordinary among a sea of ordinary. You are a dreamer and a realist all rolled into one. There is nothing you can't achieve. Thank you once again for delivering such warmth and honesty to the images in this book. Your talent and zest for life continues to astound me.

Here's to the third arm of our triumvirate, the incomparable Erika Raxworthy—thank you for your sharp eye and quiet determination. You are, hands down, the most creative person I know. The elegance in the way you work is matched only by your grace as a human being. I am so lucky to be on the receiving end of your immense talent.

A huge thank you to Sappho Hatzsis—the way you command the kitchen is fierce and beyond impressive. Your zen energy is very special to be around.

Huge hugs to Maria Midoes, the gentle soul who takes such powerfully evocative pictures. You have such a big future; I'm just humbled to be a small part of your present. Muchos gracias to Xochitl Adriana for your behind-the-scenes magic.

Thank you to Judy Linden at Stonesong for your bright smiles and unwavering optimism. I truly value your guidance, professionalism, and warmth.

Thank you to my American family at Roost Books. Sara Bercholz, it was genuinely endearment at first sight. Heartfelt thanks to you, and to the lovely Jennifer Urban-Brown, for your belief in my story of food, family, and friendship. It has been an utter pleasure working with the wonderful folks at Shambhala Publications and Roost Books.

I'm so lucky to have Mary Small on my side. Thank you for your insight, sagacity, kindness, and friendship. Working with you makes my heart swell with happiness. Big thanks also to the charming Clare Marshall, my indomitable publicist Charlotte Ree, and everyone at Plum Books and Pan Macmillan Australia for making this all happen.

Thank you to my very gracious and clever art director Daniel New—working with you has been a joy. Thanks also to my editor Simon Davis.

Thank you to all my sweet-makers scattered around the globe for sharing your friendship and sweet genius—Jennifer Wong, Charlotte Ree, Bianca Presto, Erika Raxworthy, Wesley Verhoeve, Ron and Leetal Arazi, Jodi Moreno, and Samantha Hillman.

I wanted to say a special thank you to the people of Surry Hills, where this offbeat story all began—I may be gone, but you're not forgotten.

Thank you to my dearest friend Davida Sweeney for your weekly phone calls from the Antipodes—your voice, your wise words, and, most of all, your friendship mean the world to me.

Thank you to friends near and far who relentlessly support me on this salad adventure: Matt Lennon, Joanne Solomon, Linsey Laidlaw, Shirley Cai, Katia Kelly, Stephen Lipuma, Amy Ng, Melanie Hansche, Jason Hoy, Lorraine Abela, Irma Gunadi, and Gabi Wynhausen.

Thank you to the amazing Robert Gordon family for your generosity—your plates take my salads to a whole new level of pretty! Thank you also to the amazing folk at Staub, Brooklyn Slate, and Utopia Goods.

Thank you to my family: my mother Lindy who raised us with the smell of ginger on her hands and wonderful food on the table every night. Thank you to my big sister Letty and big brother Kerby for keeping things real.

My heart belongs to my little peeps—Scout, Dash, and Huck—after all these years, I still can't choose which one of you is my favorite, so you'll have to settle for sharing the title. Thank you for agreeing to eat the salads I dish up so regularly, and with smiles on your faces too!

This book is dedicated to my husband. This salad commotion couldn't happen without him at my side. Simply, he is so rad.

—HM

INDEX

Index

Roost Books
An imprint of Shambhala Publications, Inc.
4720 Walnut Street
Boulder, Colorado 80301
roostbooks.com

Food preparation by Sappho Hatzsis and Hetty McKinnon
Prop and food styling by Erika Raxworthy
Props provided by Robert Gordon Australia, Staub, Utopia Goods, and Zwilling J. A. Henckels.

9 8 7 6 5 4 3 2 1

First U.S. Edition
Printed in China

⊗This edition is printed on acid-free paper that meets the American National
Standards Institute Z39.48 Standard.
♻Shambhala makes every effort to print on recycled paper.
For more information please visit www.shambhala.com.

Distributed in the United States by Penguin Random House LLC and in Canada by
Random House of Canada Ltd

Library of Congress Cataloging-in-Publication Data
Names: McKinnon, Hetty, author.
Title: Neighborhood: hearty salads and plant-based recipes from home and abroad / Hetty McKinnon.
Other titles: Neighbourhood
Description: First edition. | Boulder: Roost Books, 2017. | First published in 2016 by Pan Macmillan
Australia Pty Limited, Sydney, Australia. | Includes index.
Identifiers: LCCN 2016040133 | ISBN 9781611804553 (paperback)
Subjects: LCSH: Salads. | Desserts. | BISAC: COOKING / Courses & Dishes / Salads. | COOKING /
Vegetarian & Vegan. | COOKING / Specific Ingredients / Natural Foods. | LCGFT: Cookbooks.
Classification: LCC TX807 .M39 2017 | DDC 641.83—dc23 LC record available at https://lccn.loc.
gov/2016040133